Long Branch, New Jersey
Reinventing a Resort

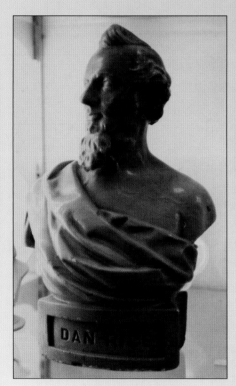

Randall Gabriel

Schiffer Publishing Ltd

4880 Lower Valley Road, Atglen, Pennsylvania 19310

Copyright © 2009 by Randall Gabrielan
Library of Congress Control Number: 2009930488

Designed by Mark David Bowyer
Type set in Aldine 721 BT / Zurich BT

ISBN: 978-0-7643-3366-8
Printed in China

Contents

SCENE ON PLEASURE BAY, LONG BRANCH, N. J.

Acknowledgments

This book was made possible by the many people who contributed vintage images that make the past come alive. The first thanks goes to John Rhody and Glenn Vogel, who offered pictures years ago with the confidence that they would help bring history to the public. Karen L. Schnitzspahn merits special thanks not only because so many of her contributions are significant additions to the book, but because she lent information from the core of her own historical work. Daniel Hennessey was a skilled photographer and collector of vintage prints. His work is represented through two sources, his widow Gloria and Gail Gannon, who has custody of many images and has long been a supporter of the author.

Gail Hari has helped in so many ways, as a springboard for ideas, in reading pieces of the manuscript, in printing imagery, and for miscellaneous advice and counsel. Thanks, Gail. Two sources with deep roots in the city were always around to take a question and provide some insight: Arthur Green, whose family once owned much of the southern part of Long Branch, and Beth Woolley. Thank you to both. The Long Branch Public Library has been helpful through the provision of images, reference material, and access to their resources. Thanks to the organization, their staff, and guardian of the local history room, Elsalyn Palmisano.

The author has long-believed that contributions from many help make a better book. Thanks go to all those who provided one or more images, including: Joseph Carney, the late Aileen Connolly, the late Elene Dwyer, W. Edmund Kemble, Kathi McGrath, Dean Marchetto, George Moss, Rutgers Special Collections and University Archives, Robert Schoeffling, Keith Wells, and Joseph Dangler for his research on Bath. Other images are owned by the author, who took the contemporary photographs.

This plate from the 1905 Survey Map Company Atlas of New Jersey depicts a Long Branch that is much longer than it is wide. The atlas, which was endorsed by the new American Automobile Association, focused on roads, but one of this image's more interesting features is the three intersecting railroad lines. Only the one marked "NY&LB" survives and all stations except Long Branch on Third Avenue are gone. Most of the depicted churches stand, albeit some with significant change. Most of the top of the map should be blue to reflect the Shrewsbury River, but depicting the geography beyond the borders was beyond the intent of the map-maker.

LONG BRANCH
Monmouth Co. N.J.

Introduction

The essentials of the career of Long Branch are so well-known that they have become shopworn through familiarity. Understanding of the city's rich and complex history has become eroded by old interpretations, which at best have grown stale and at worst are wrong. The brevity and hollowness of glamour and gambling should not dominate a rich and complex history. It is true that moneyed classes of post-Civil War America enjoyed new socializing at shorefront ballrooms, while gaming halls attracted high rollers with personas as wide as their wads. They created two Long Branches, separate and unequal, permanent and transient. After access to Long Branch became democratized through new and improved transportation, the affluent decided to separate from the resort's *hoi polloi* by migrating to the city's southern parts, which effectively made Long Branch two places united by a corporate commission. This volume's new insights suggest that preoccupation with the elements of the 1870s era of elegance obscures the full history of the resort, that the local impact of ocean travel was inverse to the joy of the trip, and that the loss of gambling was to the betterment of the city. Also presented with regrettable brevity is the city's early 20th century reinvention as a family resort, business hub, and population center.

By the 1860s, the patronage and popularity of Long Branch raised its stature to become the most prominent seashore resort in the East. In 2008, its present incarnation is moving to a high-rise, seashore, residential city. A century and a half ago, an ascendant Long Branch was becoming fixed as one of Monmouth County's most storied places. In 2008, historians struggle to retain its historic vestiges, to convince a populace that history matters, and to share the caring. A century and a half ago, Long Branch was home to two hostile groups: part-time summer residents who raised property values and year-round dwellers whose fiscal practices often accrued to the permanent residents rather than the common good. In 2008, there is a perception that the needs of developers prevail over the needs of the people. This book, within the constraints of text that can accompany 350 images, traces the rise and fall of the resort and touches the contemporary scene.

This linen "large letter" post card is distinguished by picturing actual places. "Branch" is bracketed by the Church of the Presidents and Our Lady, Star of the Sea.

Location and Governance

Long Branch, so-named by the first half of the 18th century for its locale south of the "long branch" of the Shrewsbury River, had as its eastern border an appealing bluff over the Atlantic Ocean, which helped to propel an early resort industry. A distinction between inland and oceanfront was made at least as early as 1834 by Gordon, when the former was a small village east of its namesake stream, while the latter was a "well-known and much frequented sea-bathing place" that possessed many "inducements to the invalid, the idle and the hunters of pleasure to spend a portion of the hot season." The shore soared in the ensuing decades, while the small village grew modestly. Their relationship became more like hostile foreign powers than parts of the same place.

The Long Branch area, initially part of one of Monmouth County' original townships, Shrewsbury, became part of Ocean Township at the latter's 1849 formation. At its peak of prominence, Long Branch's regional connotation spread beyond its future municipal boundaries; for example, the Long Branch colony of entertainers who lived outside its borders, typically in Ocean Township. One of the region's greatest estates, Shadow Lawn, and one of its most exclusive communities, Norwood Park, were within the Long Branch social and economic orbit but were located in Eatontown Township, only later in the future borough of West Long Branch. Chapter 5 examines the concept of Long Branch beyond its borders. The massive growth of property values led to a desire for greater local control. Local rule by a commission within the township was attained in 1867.

Long Branch enjoyed considerable self-governance as a commission, its status until incorporation as a city in 1903 (and reincorporation in 1904), but local and sectional rivalries continued. The administrative center was the downtown business district, while key long-term issues were erosion of the bluff and the condition of Ocean Avenue. Seasonal residents accused the authorities of using their substantial tax base to run the city year-round, while the commission countered that the shore property owners should assume greater responsibility for protecting their property. The division of Monmouth County, notably the shore, into an excessive number of small municipalities makes a travesty of New Jersey's cherished home-rule governance. However, some suggested divisions were resisted. These included a proposed splitting of the shore section from the remainder of the County in 1883 and a proposed separation of Long Branch south of Bath Avenue in 1886.

Becoming a Resort

Patronage drawn from both Philadelphia and New York was shaped in large part by the challenges of travel. The local lodging industry began with boarding houses, often residences of farmers who rented rooms seasonally. While few details survive, it is evident that boarding houses expanded into hotels, some literally. By the middle of the 19th century, Long Branch was a resort of major substance.

Long Branch's ascendance probably peaked in the 1870s. An excellent depiction of Long Branch rising, Schenck's 1868 *Album,* combines descriptive depth, promotional enthusiasm, and photographic breadth. By then, hotels had sprawled along the shore like wooden boxes on an old Monopoly board, while summer cottages built by gentlemen were sprouting around the city. The area projected architectural evolution in the rise of Stick and Second Empire style houses, prior to the latter's becoming a national craze. A cottage meant a temporary home, in addition to the common current definition, which obviates the need to place the term within quotation marks. While large summer houses were surely cottages, some latter 19th century references call anything in Long Branch not a hotel a cottage, typically the guest buildings rented by hotels to visitors who then dined in hotel halls.

Early high-tone visitors brought Long Branch elegance, money, and stature. Newport, Rhode Island was the only of its few rivals located on the shore. Prestigious but inland Saratoga then bore no comparison. In time, Long Branch's complexion evolved as populism diluted the elegance. The mix devolved as travel options expanded. The railroad and notably the ocean pier steamers, brought day-trippers who absorbed the seashore atmosphere without resting their heads here. Indeed, in the pier's planning stage, skeptics warned, "be careful of what you wish for." Still, news columns continued to enumerate new arrivals, including names dotted with the prominent, even presidents. The changed social mix that evolved with new travel facilities is a compelling subject that merits deeper study.

A major change of Long Branch's character ensued in the early 1880s. Rail access, which initially required a preliminary steamer trip, was facilitated considerably by the "all-land route" and opening of the Central Depot in 1875, at the present New Jersey Transit station location. This, combined with the building of an ocean pier in 1879, helped "democratize" the place's social mix. Historical recollection of the pier is rooted through romantic imagery, but in reality the pier was the worst man-made object for wrecking the resort's exclusivity.

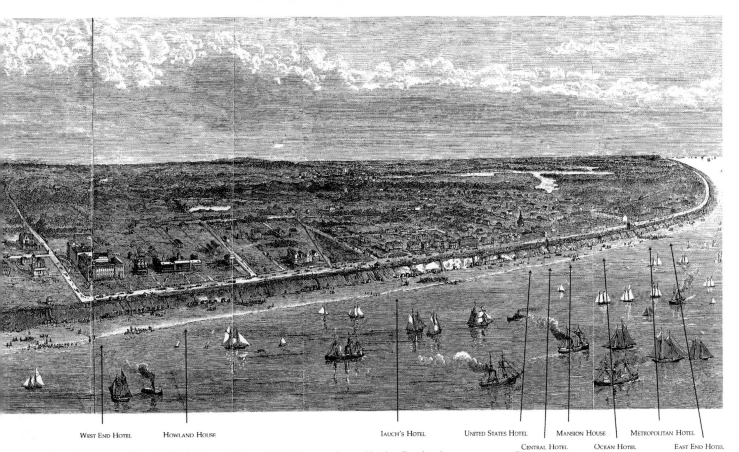

WEST END HOTEL HOWLAND HOUSE IAUCH'S HOTEL UNITED STATES HOTEL MANSION HOUSE METROPOLITAN HOTEL
CENTRAL HOTEL OCEAN HOTEL EAST END HOTEL

This print, originally in the *Harper's Weekly* issue of August 23, 1873, was enhanced by the directional arrows that appeared in its reprint in Moss and Schnitzspahn.

Siperstein Paints moved from its long-time lower Broadway location, which has been planned as Long Branch's art zone, to 700 Joline Avenue, in the city's northwest, where that stem is also known as Highway 36. They hired noted artist Bob Mataranglo to make a distinctive image on their east façade and parking lot entrance. Bob, noted for his murals, painted *Broadway 1939*, his chef d'oeuvre, with the assistance of Tom De Angelo. This major segment of the massive work is framed by two images found elsewhere in the book, the Garfield statue at the right, and at left, a view of Broadway looking west, which in Chapter 2 is pictured on a postcard.

While steamers helped fill hotels near the dock and provided a pleasant alternative ride in suitable weather, for the most part they brought too many ill-mannered, parsimonious day-trippers in numbers that congested the place with little impact on its economy. Their marring the northern resort area sent the upper echelon towards Long Branch's edges, including Elberon, West End, Hollywood, and Norwood Park; the movement is recounted in Chapters 3 and 5.

Horse racing and gambling have a storied and important, but not fully-studied role in Long Branch history. At its 1870 opening, the original Monmouth Park was a glamorous recreational addition. Early success is reflected in the track's expansion and following as a "sporting" venue for many of the wealthy. However, the lower element soon diminished the glamour, while the park endured for less than a quarter-century. It was quashed after the 1893 season by a statewide anti-gambling movement led locally by pious, but racist, James A. Bradley of Asbury Park. At the end, the park's significance was marginalized as the region's racing activity was centered in New York City (not Saratoga). The loss of horse racing as a factor in the resort's decline is not exaggerated; it is wrong. The dismal Long Branch 1893 season was due, in part, to a national recession. Improvement the next year stemmed further decline through the onset of the horse show at Hollywood and the overall better crowd drawn by that equine exhibition. Actually, the major cause of the resort's fall was the slow rot that set-in with a complacent hotel ownership, which did nothing to improve its aging stock. The dismal boxes, pictured when relatively new in Chapter 2, were largely still around in 1893, but were well-along in a process of destruction by neglect, demolition, or fire that was completed early in the new century. News accounts that describe the success of the seasons following 1893 refute assertions that horse racing in its later years was a significant economic factor in Long Branch.

Gambling

The gambling house issue has a different complexion. Gaming clubs were built here for the urban affluent in order to capture the summer business of a New York-Philadelphia clientele that fled the sweltering cities. Lack of legality had hardly been an impediment to this high-rolling action until legislation stiffened in 1905 that made local officials liable for failure to enforce the law in the face of known gambling activity. That closed the clubs. They were shut. Terminated. Their owners obviously understood the message as they shipped their gambling apparatus to New York. The newly-enlightened officials of the recently incorporated city were then faced with an even greater challenge: reinventing Long Branch as a family resort. Timing was poor as the infrastructure rot had deepened and another recession loomed in 1907. The need to end long-illegal gambling through a legislative remedy suggests local connivance and corruption that would plague city government for decades. This vital and critical subject is beyond the ambit of this work.

Recovery

Long Branch addressed the new century's challenges by building Ocean Park (see Chapter 2), becoming a manufacturing center, and improving Ocean Avenue. The contentious history of the city's primary waterfront included encroachments by property owners and the avenue's lay-out in varying widths; design flaws made the road an inconsistent and inconvenient thoroughfare. Subsequent improvements made Ocean Avenue such an effective roadway in the emerging interstate motoring era that the city suffered an unintended consequence by 1930. Then, shore visitors, attracted by better regional roads and water crossings, could race through Long Branch to resorts emerging in southern Monmouth County.

The frequent presence of seven United States presidents helped to elevate Long Branch's stature. Presidential notoriety was actually first made by a spouse, Mary Todd Lincoln, whose 1861 celebrated visit helped raise Long Branch's profile. One president resided here during the summer. Ulysses S. Grant was drawn by friends who calculated correctly his value to the city; they installed him in his own seaside villa. The sad tale of James A. Garfield's dieing in Elberon has been told often. Taken to Long Branch for the salubrious seaside environment, with hope it would aid recovery from an assailant's bullet, his succumbing at the Franklyn Cottage made that place a veritable shrine. While Shadow Lawn, the temporary home of president Woodrow Wilson, was then part of the new borough of West Long Branch, Long Branch interests motivated his coming in 1916 to benefit the resort. His re-election campaign from his summer White House front porch became part of presidential lore. The other U. S. presidents who stayed here are recounted in Chapter 3.

Several pictures had multiple prospective places in this book. Some may appear to be out of geographical position because they were placed in relevant historical sequence.

Chapter 1.
Northern Long Branch
Including Branchport and Pleasure Bay

Northern Long Branch conveniently links a once-amorphous area located north of the hotel district and south of the Wardell farm. Some parts were known by now-obscure names that reflected local character, such as Fish Town and Shell Dock. Branchport and Pleasure Bay, located downriver on the Shrewsbury's "long branch," were once, for practical purposes, separate places. When Monmouth Beach was being developed in the late 19th century, there was often little distinction between its south and the north of Long Branch. The coming of the railroads and the establishment of post offices placed names on the land, including East Long Branch, North Long Branch, and Atlanticville, areas linked in this chapter.

Northern Long Branch was virtually a microcosm of the city at large, but also had its distinctions. Its presence on Branchport Creek and Pleasure Bay made Northern Long Branch a gateway to the ocean shore, while maritime interests also included a modest shipbuilding industry.

Northern Long Branch, which fronts on the ocean, once had seashore hotels and recreational facilities, a role now recalled by the popular Seven Presidents Oceanfront Park. It had been a rail center and still has a business district, although the latter was rended by the building of the New Ocean Boulevard over the former rail right-of-way. While older houses still dotted its landscape, Northern Long Branch was chosen for an investment colony of better houses, called Nate Salsbury's Reservation, built here in the early 20th century. The several names on the land in Northern Long Branch are explained in the picture captions, but two stand out. Pleasure Bay and Branchport were once destinations in their own right. Now they have virtually disappeared from the landscape, their resort and dock character effaced. Northern Long Branch, as does the entire city, faces a challenge of preserving its historic character.

The legendary Price's Hotel, which opened in 1854, was famed for its bountiful table, notably for "shore dinners", an assemblage of seafood and meats that spelled "excess" wonderfully in the latter 19th and early 20th centuries. While Capt. Edward H. Price was the original owner, his wife Ann's food preparation brought the place its renown. Price's, a restaurant only in its latter years, early-on attracted the rich, famous and politically well-connected or elected. It was said that favor by President Grant cultivated Price's reputation among the powerful set. Located on the Shrewsbury River, much of its early trade came by steamer. Price's, which was particularly busy during the original Monmouth Park's racing season, was closed by fire on November 8, 1953, eight years after this image by W. Edmund Kemble.

Surviving parts of the built environment make this c.1950 aerial readily identifiable. However, the scene's greatest change is the New Ocean Boulevard, built in the 1980s over the roadbed of the former Central Railroad (New Jersey Southern), a concrete band, which split the community far greater than had the railroad. A piece of the old Ocean Avenue is at lower right. The three large identifiable buildings that form a triangle in the center are the Methodist Church with its steeply pitched roof, the large-box Church Street School and the Presley Garage with the hipped roof. Numerous older surviving houses and several business buildings, along with the Oliver Byron Fire Company, give North Long Branch the character of community.

The Pleasure Bay Bridge, or O-29 for its Monmouth County number, connects Monmouth Boulevard, Oceanport with Long Branch's Port au Peck Avenue. This swing bridge, which was built in 1883, was demolished for the 1965 construction of the 25 foot high concrete arch bridge located a few feet east of the pictured span, or on a path through the edge of the destroyed Price's. The undated image is likely second quarter of the 20th century.

The Hotel Norwood, pictured on a c.1910 post card, at 336 Branchport Avenue on Branchport Creek, Pleasure Bay, was built c.1866 as the DeNyse Hotel. Changing names and incarnations from time to time, it has been a popular restaurant for the past quarter century and looks less and less its familiar post card imagery, although the building's outlines can still be detected in 2008 under extensive change. The roundhouse gazebo disappeared long ago, as the intersecting Atlantic Avenue became a major thoroughfare. (Courtesy of Keith Wells)

The Queen Anne style Bridgewater Inn, pictured on a c.1915 post card, was located at the entrance to Pleasure Bay Park opposite Price's. Situated on Branchport Creek, steamers brought a city patronage for the place's amusement rides and picnic facilities. Private residences on Atlantic Avenue are on the site.

Long Branch's southern bridge over Branchport Creek, No. E-20, which crosses that stream on Branchport Avenue, is visible in the right background of the companion hotel picture. The span pictured on a c.1907 post card was likely built in 1896, replaced in 1944 and again by the present span in 1985. That new bridge remains nearly level with the road as navigation, except for the smallest craft, effectively ends at this point.

The steamship *Mary Patten*, built in Brooklyn in 1893 and rebuilt there in 1900, sailed out of Pleasure Bay for a career that endured until 1931. Her registered length and breadth were 182 and 28.1 feet respectively, while she drew 7.8 feet. The vessel's 508 gross tonnage embraced a carrying capacity of 130 tons; her crew was 14. The ship suffered late-career financial hardship; the statistics were lifted from a Bill of Sale of Enrolled Vessel following a 1928 auction sale to the Second National Bank and Trust Co., which had foreclosed its mortgage. The *Mary Patten* started rotting at her dock after it ceased running in 1931. The demolition and ruins clearance took about 15 years.

GREEN GABLES, Pleasure Bay, N. J. NICHOLAS E. WEST, Prop.

Nicholas E. West, after long service fishing out of Sea Bright, retired to the less hazardous career of running a resort on Pleasure Bay. Green Gables was located on the north bank, evidence that Pleasure Bay spanned the Long Branch border with the future Oceanport.

An active boat-building business developed on Branchport Creek, notably the Seaman Sea Skiff Works at 491 Atlantic Avenue, a four-generation firm founded in Sea Bright around 1851. The *New Jersey* appears to be what Harold Seaman recalled as one of their biggest jobs from early in the 20th century, three 60-foot steam powered boats that cruised the Navesink and Shrewsbury Rivers as "aquatic jitneys." Harold, who also claimed the founding date, closed the business in 1960 when his property was taken for urban renewal.

The Patten Point Yacht Club, founded around 1964 is headquartered in the 1895 former Thomas G. Patten house on Patten Avenue at the mouth of Manahassett Creek. The club drew its initials members from the Monmouth Power Boat Association, led by key founder Dr. Martin R. Rush. A glimpse of their fleet is pictured in 1979.

Newbolds Woods, located on the Shrewsbury River and also known as Branchport Woods, was a popular picnic grounds, but also was reported to be a refuge for gypsies. While the memory has faded, the place's then-significance can be inferred from this full-page illustration in a 1907 Long Branch souvenir booklet.

The bridge scene on a c.1915 post card is likely Troutmans Creek, although the landscape is hardly recognizable nearly a century later. That bridge was replaced in 1925 by one subsequently replaced by the present No. O-35 in 2007.

This six-foot granite monument, which honors the namesake of Martin Luther King Memorial Park, was erected by Peaceable Kingdom Memorials and dedicated in January 2002. The park's site, located at Atlantic Avenue and Atlantic Drive, was chosen for its serene surroundings as a place where a visitor could reflect and relax. The Martin Luther King Memorial Guild, formed at the city's Second Baptist Church, oversaw the project, which was paid for by a number of contributions and fundraisers. One of four quotations is visible on this 2007 view looking west. The side with the King portrait states, "Every man is somebody because he is a child of God."

Simon Baruch, 1840-1921, served in the Confederate Army after graduating in 1862 from the Medical College of Virginia. He wrote extensively on medical matters, was a pioneer of scientific hydrotherapy, became expert in the surgical treatment of gunshot wounds and was consulted widely on chronic cases, his special expertise. His 395 Atlantic Avenue estate, which backed on the Shrewsbury River, was earlier known as Doerrhurst for the prior owner, John Doerr. The house predating Doerr, who owned the property from 1895-1903, is inferred stylistically as a Second Empire house remodeled as a Queen Anne. Pictured on a c.1912 post card, the house's sometimes association with Hartwig, one of Simon's four sons, may stem from the former's name appearing on another card, or his mooring a substantial yacht here (the likely inspiration for *Anchorage*), or since the Baruchs used the place as a family compound. Herman Benjamin Baruch took title May 1, 1903, then promptly deeded the property to Belle, Simon's wife, who retained it until April 11, 1918. Four owners held the property over the next decade, one naming itself Anchorage Realty Co., before it passed to the Northern Baptist University of New Jersey, a Newark organization that used it briefly to train African American clergy. The house was destroyed by fire in June 1961; housing now fills the site. (Courtesy of Karen L. Schnitzspahn)

This house appears to have been expanded so often as to obscure its origin or style. Labeled "W.E.D. Stokes" on this c.1907 post card, the Atlantic Avenue house was begun by Andrew Gilsey who owned the property for much of the late 19th century. Stokes' life was shaped as much by misery as by the fortune left him by his father. The 1874 Yale graduate married the teenage celebrated beauty Rita de Allen Acosta in 1895 after falling in love with her picture in a window. Life following their 1900 divorce was characterized by litigation, marital problems, a clash with the New York City Health Department over pigs kept at his Hotel Ansonia and great bodily harm as a consequence of a dispute with chorus girl associates. His attempt at authorship was repelling. The eugenics book *The Right to Be Well Born* suggested registering the family history of the laboring class to determine their potential value as workers. Following his death at age 73 in 1926, the property was sold for development of the small houses of Narragansett Park. (*New York Times,* May 20, 1926)

Each destruction of a noteworthy vintage building is a heartfelt loss in Long Branch where time, neglect and indifference have decimated the built environment. The c.1890s Edgar A. West Building reflected the former vibrancy of the North Long Branch business district. An appealing façade with the building name in the cornice gave the store and apartment distinction and even historic stature. It was the first building listed in the Monmouth County Historic Sites Inventory, a placement admittedly alphabetic from its 28 Atlantic Avenue address. The early 1980s construction of the New Ocean Boulevard split the area, leaving the east to a future of multiple dwellings and its short stem of Atlantic Avenue virtually an island. The building was demolished in 2008; the image dates from 1994.

The North Long Branch station on the New Jersey Southern line (successor to the 1865 Long Branch and Seashore Railroad) was off the northeast corner of Atlantic Avenue and New Ocean Boulevard, across both streets from the pictured West and Presley buildings. Indeed, the latter street was built along its roadbed. Little of the c.1890s structure is visible in this undated photograph in which station agent Daniel I. Hennessey, Sr. is seated to the left of the trunk in the center.

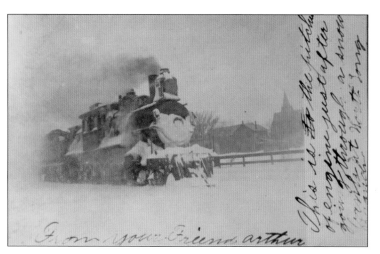

One might excuse Arthur's spelling after considering how often the word "picture" has been mispronounced. The back of this photographic post card reveals a February 9, 1907 postmark from North Long Branch. (Courtesy of Glenn Vogel)

William G. Presley had established a bicycle shop at 45 Atlantic Avenue at least by 1912. As the lettering in this c.1920s photograph suggests, he expanded into a machine shop and garage. In time, he also sold gasoline.

The former Presley garage is obscured by later additions and alterations. A former exterior wall runs through the middle of the structure which earlier in 2008 had been vacant and reportedly part of a major real estate legal issue. A garage operation endured into the 1980s, a period when the building was included in the Monmouth County Historic Sites Inventory. There it was later prematurely listed as "demolished." The report of its death is an exaggeration as Mark Twain once noted following publication of an obituary in his lifetime. This 2008 photograph provides the evidence. A new restaurant was opening at year's end.

Philadelphia architect Charles W. Bolton designed the Romanesque Revival Asbury Methodist Episcopal Church at 61 Atlantic Avenue, the northeast corner of Church Street. Built in 1894 and pictured in 2008, this edifice replaced a frame church dating from 1872. The pyramidal roof that had topped the tower was removed in a c.1945 rebuilding project necessitated to correct structural defects. An extension built in 1898 on the north fits seamlessly with the original structure.

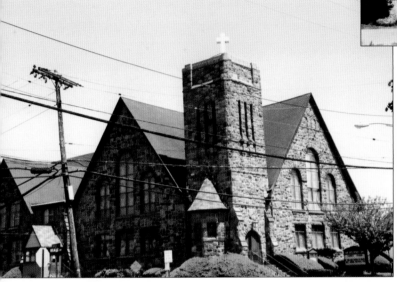

The Benjamin White house at 464 Church Street, one of the city's oldest, is believed to date from the first quarter of the 19th century. Moved from across the street when the North Long Branch School was built, the house is named for the White who inherited the property from his father in 1825 and lived there until his 1882 death. The 1 ½ story section on the north may be the oldest. The two room addition on the rear of the two-story main block, reportedly added in the late 1940s to accommodate a doctor's office, was designed by Freehold architect J. Hallam Conover, along with other colonial revival modifications. This image of the well-preserved house dates from 1994.

While its educational career ended in 1978, the battered, vacant and neglected former North Long Branch School still attained National Register of Historic Places listing in 1999. This building at 469 Church Street is a twin of the Broadway School pictured in Chapter 4. Built in 1881 by C.V.N. Wilson (per plaque) and Garrett Hennessey (per building contract), the smaller section in front was the original structure. The school was expanded twice, in 1900 and following fire damage in 1929, presumably the two-story and one-story extensions respectively. The building, which once had an attic floor with a pitched roof, is pictured in 1994. In the 1990s, the Long Branch Historical Association had planned to refurbish the building for museum use, a project abandoned for reasons of cost and practicality. Changes by 2008 included the fencing-off of the property, the boarding of its windows and sundry signs of decline.

It is believed that Russell Maps, the richest man in Long Branch in his time, founded the lumber and building materials dealer that became known as Chandler and Maps by about 1888. While their address was 64 South Broadway, the firm occupied a block-long yard along the former New Jersey Southern (Central) tracks. The firm, which was owned by A. Chandler and T.L. Maps by the turn of the 20th century, endured for over a century as an active participant in Long Branch's greatest period of expansion. The image, while possessing a number of dating hints, is only estimated as latter 1920s. (Courtesy of Glenn Vogel)

The large Chandler & Maps yard contained a mill and extensive storage facilities. This collection of older, vernacular business buildings, which had attained historic stature by the late 20th century, was destroyed by fire in September, 1991. (Courtesy of Glenn Vogel)

The Reservation

Nathan Salsbury, born in Illinois around 1845, joined the Union army as a youth where he reportedly honed his singing, dancing and card playing skills. He was said to have left the service with $20,000 accumulated through poker playing. He discovered his theatrical aptitude in Grand Rapids, Michigan, bounced around the stage for a while before landing a four year stint as a comedian at the Boston Museum, where he played with other rising stars. Salsbury, known as Nate, founded Salsbury's Troubadours, a company that traveled extensively throughout the U.S. and Europe. He was so-engaged when he met Col. William Cody; they launched the popular "Buffalo Bill's Wild West Show." The peripatetic Salsbury, who needed a home base, chose Long Branch, a city where he had regularly visited his manager, Frank Maeder. (*Times,* August 5, 1883) Nate bought the lot adjacent to Maeder in 1882 and it appears the two had adjacent houses at 321 and 323 Liberty Street, although no vintage house survives on either lot. He also purchased the site of the former

East End Hotel in 1900, a 16 and 2/3 acre parcel that he divided into 14 lots for his house colony known as The Reservation. The long-vacant premises had been earlier owned by Jay Gould and later John Hoey, who failed to realize plans for a major hotel. Thus, Salsbury's development was welcomed in the area as it countered recent neglect.

The nearby shore, buffeted by storms, had been eroding, while the hotels were in a state of decline. One can only presume Salsbury's intentions were investment income, perhaps to support retirement. He reportedly planned to build in 1900-01 about eleven houses designed by Leon Cubberley, typically in the Queen Anne or Shingle Styles, but it appears that only nine were constructed. Each was given an Indian name and also identified by a number. Most were east of Ocean Avenue; shore lots were separated by a private road known as "The Trail." They included:

No. 1, Cheyenne
No. 2, Iroquois
No. 3, Navaho
No. 4, Arapahoe

This Historic American Buildings Survey c. 1930s photograph is of an unidentified Reservation house.

No. 5, Uncaspapa
No. 6, Okalhofee
No. 7, Cherokee
No. 8, Okelsska
No. 9, Miami.

Salsbury did not endure to enjoy ownership of the pride of North Long Branch; he died December 24, 1902. His widow, who retained the Reservation for nearly two decades, sold the last of the houses in 1920. She inserted a number of deed restrictions; one barred fences unless under four feet in height and of an ornamental nature. Over the decades, the houses suffered a slow, steady decline. Three had been lost by 1970, a time when public use of the property was contemplated by the Long Branch Community Development body. Complicated proceedings beyond the ambit of this work subsequently placed the property with the Monmouth County Park System. The one remaining salvageable house, the Navaho, was moved from its original location and preserved. Other deteriorated houses were demolished.

Only one of the six Reservation houses that survived to the era of public ownership was considered for saving. They were in deteriorated condition. Also, how many houses were needed in a park? The demolition was in August 1980.

Recreational development of the area, part of the Long Branch Master Plan of 1965, was expected to herald the rebirth of the city, although critics claimed the park project's size exceeded the needs of the city. Thus, it appears fitting that the Reservation passed into the county's stewardship as it now stands as one of their system's most visited parks. The preserved "Navaho", pictured in 2006, serves as the headquarters of Seven Presidents Oceanfront Park, which occupies most of the former Reservation.

Noted actor Oliver Doud Byron, eventually owned about eleven houses on both sides of the Monmouth Beach border with the city, holding many for rental income. See the bibliography's William J. Busby for a detailed account of the showman's career and local property activity. Busby, who lives in this house at 476 Neptune Avenue, notes that while it was here called *Byron's Bower*, the house was also known as *Honeysuckle Lodge.* He also tells of Byron's use of recycled materials, including the pentagonal windows removed from Grant's cottage after remodeling, visible on the façade in this c.1910 post card. (Courtesy of John Rhody)

A fine row of houses on the west side of Ocean Avenue, north of Avenel Boulevard, pictured on a c.1910 post card, reflects North Long Branch's summer home era. Later they were occupied by the Salvation Army Fresh Air program that brought urban children to the shore for respites from the sweltering city. Their origin may date from the 1909 inheritance of the Murray Cottage at the corner of Atlantic Avenue. That summer, local residents petitioned the Salvation Army to cease their recreational use of the place claiming it lowered property values. (*Times,* September 22, 1909) Time has taken a toll on this strip. (Courtesy of Karen L. Schnitzspahn)

The Evangeline by the Sea Hotel, earlier the Sea Shore Cottage but renamed for Evangeline Booth, daughter of William, of the Salvation Army, is pictured on a c.1940 post card during their operation. Due to a New York polio epidemic in 1916, the Salvation Army was barred from bringing to its vacation retreats mothers and children. Perhaps this was the origin of the hotel becoming a vacation home for working girls. Much of that week's population appears to be posing, mainly lounging, but some showing their varied recreational activities.

This c.1910 post card view looks south on the east side of Ocean Avenue from just south of the Monmouth Beach border, to Atlantic Avenue. The northern edge of Seven Presidents Oceanfront Park would later exist behind the houses in the distance. Busby tells of Byron's ownership of three of the houses. His start on the shore was *Castle Byron,* a no-longer extant house at 459 Ocean, here one to the right of the open lot. Byron and wife Mary Kate built the third and fourth houses from the left, the still-extant numbers 469 and 465, naming the former *Surfside.* The Evangeline by the Sea would be closer to the shore behind the cottages at the rear.

The *Times* (July 29) claimed at the time of the 1910 sale of the Arthur B. Proal house to William A. Jamison of Arbuckle Bros., "This is considered one of the finest places on the Jersey Coast." It was on the ocean in Monmouth Beach, making the image the west façade. While the 1893 expansion of the Queen Anne style house likely included the tower and wing on the south, or right, the place's origins are obscure. Examination of deeds leads one to conclude the house was built by Frank and Celine Hollins. Their 1880 purchase of the lot from investors for $258 was presumably for vacant land, while their 1882 sale for $12,000 to Jane L. Thomson presumably included a house. The dwelling, about 450 feet south of Valentine Street and located on the site of the borough's municipal beach, came down at an unknown date. (Courtesy of George Moss)

The 1894 development Mannahassett Park linked the Valentine Street area of Monmouth Beach and northern Long Branch via a bridge over Mannahassett Bay. While the Long Branch section, located between Bay and Long Branch Avenues, north of Colonia Drive, was the smaller, a map issued for the 1919 liquidation sale of the Life Insurance Company of Virginia indicated comparable development in each section. The hotel was in Long Branch, the slogan on the c.1905 post card notwithstanding, located just north of the bridge that once connected the parts. (Courtesy of Michael Steinhorn)

Fishermen from northern Long Branch had long sent their boats into the surf from a stretch of Wardell's narrow barrier beach. While they had the owner's concurrence, they foresaw that this arrangement might not survive the Wardell estate's sale. Thus, they pooled funds to buy a $500 lot from Arthur V. Conover in 1870, transferring title in 1884 to the Galilee Fishing Association. Their simple craft, a Sea Bright skiff enlarged to about a 50-foot length with a 10-foot beam, typically required a crew of six and a team of horses to beach a fish-laden boat. This one, the *Ann Marie,* owned by Sam Sicilliano, won an amateur photographers prize for George V. Maney around 1940. (Courtesy of Gail Gannon)

The west façade of this industrial building faces Branchport Avenue at number 273, set back from the street, but still visible, located just north of the New York and Long Branch tracks. While Kay Dunhill Inc., a garment manufacturer, was here when it was photographed in August, 1952, the building was shortly thereafter occupied by Wheelock Signals, Inc. The place was recognizable in 2008 after a façade makeover, one that included the removal of the truck bay. (Dorn's Classic Images)

Chapter 2.
Central Shore
The Heart of the Branch

The mile-long row of shorefront resorts is so deeply at the core of Long Branch's significance that it is examined in depth in the book's Introduction and in this chapter's hotel segment. In short, Long Branch rose to prominence at the central shore and declined precipitously with the fading of the hotels towards the end of the 19th century. The shore survived much of the 20th century by becoming a family resort and through changing its popular pastimes. The central shore also was in the fore of Long Branch's transformation to a high-rise residential city late in the 20th century. A number of successful projects have risen here at the end of 2008. Pier Village, perhaps the most successful of them, has become a destination in its own right. However, the area is also riven by development disputes that cloud the central shore's future. In addition, the 2008 economic downturn and the collapse of the real estate market brought challenges shared by the rest of the state and country.

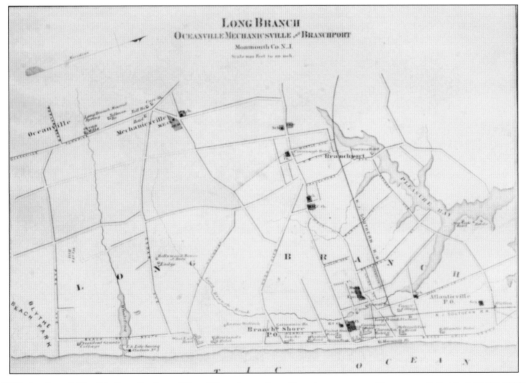

In 1872, the date of this plate from the Beers Atlas of New Jersey, Long Branch was governed by a commission technically within Ocean Township. Oceanville and Mechanicsville, the two villages at top, were also part of the township. Blythe Beach Park at the left was a forerunner of Elberon. The hotels at the bottom are reviewed in Chapter 2. The New Jersey Southern Railroad is depicted approaching Long Branch from two directions, as the line absorbed both the region's original railroad, the Raritan and Delaware Bay, which ran through Branchport, and the Long Branch and Seashore, which ran from Sandy Hook. While "north" is traditionally oriented at top, here "north" is on the right so that the map had a shore orientation, as did all of Long Branch.

Travel to the Branch and the Pier

Cunard Lines advertised that "Getting there is half the fun," but early travel to Long Branch was anything but fun. Indeed, it was just awful. While the resort at its colonial-era origins drew visitors from New York and Philadelphia, the latter's overland trip was predictably rough over sandy, rutted paths, while the unpredictability of wind and weather made a New Yorker's trip by sail range from time-consuming to impossible. Steam-powered vessels could improve matters by making that near-impossible trip to the Shrewsbury River merely long and difficult. Later ocean docking would create new possibilities. Historic references indicate that the first ocean dock was built in 1828 around Bath Avenue at a time when Bath was promoted as a separate village. It is claimed this pier was destroyed in the November 1854 storm that destroyed the *New Era.*

While early steamers docked on the Shrewsbury River, the *Elberon* is not only a later boat, built in 1888, but this is a later image, a c.1915 post card. The craft was commissioned by the Merchant's Steamboat Company to run in opposition to the Patten Line, but it was bought by the latter to eliminate the competition. The *Elberon,* which sailed for Patten until 1920, was sold to other lines, renamed and ran until 1932. (Courtesy of Glenn Vogel)

This artist's rendering of the first pier was published by *Harper's Weekly* June 21, 1879 as the pier was opening. In popular lore, the 1879 pier was often called the "ocean pier," while the 1881 replacement is called the "iron pier." Actually, both were built of iron and "ocean pier" is a descriptive term for a pier that could dock ocean-going ships.

Long Branch's first railroad station was located a block north of lower Broadway. Reaching the shore hotels still required a short stagecoach ride. (Schenck)

The date of the sketch is unknown, but this pier rendering was the back of an 1880 timetable card for the *Plymouth Rock*, the shore's largest steamer, described as "mammoth and magnificent."

At the time of *Frank Leslie's Illustrated Newspaper's* August 22, 1857 publication of this image, the stage ride from the Shrewsbury River to the oceanfront hotel could be long and arduous At busy times, a continuous row of coaches lined the route.

The damage depicted on this Private Mailing Card (an early post card) was probably that caused by the March 1, 1900 storm. The press reported the collapse of about 50 feet of pier located about 300 feet from its end. (Courtesy of Kathi McGrath)

6   The Broken Iron Pier at Long Branch, N. J.

J. N. VAN HORN, PRINTER, 512 B'WAY LONG BRANCH, N. J.

This c.1910 post card is a rendering of a never-built second story for the new pier. The elevated structure was probably a grand concept hatched prior to engineering as the reality of construction costs and the realization that ocean travel to Long Branch was ending, would have doomed the idea prior to erection.

New Pavilion, Long Branch, N. J.

405797

Pier amusements were many, varied and changing with the times. The tower supported "airplane cars" for the Lindy Loop aerial ride. Was that attraction, pictured on a c.1920s white border post card, named for a famous aviator? Dancing enjoyed enduring popularity. (Courtesy of Kathi McGrath)

The original pier appealed to anglers from the start. An 1881 report revealed a crowd casting lines, hauling catches of black-fish, sea-bass, and blue-fish. Fishing was so well-established by 1915 that the *Times* on May 30 claimed no attraction was more popular, adding, "The pier has won a distinction all its own since it is the only public pleasure centre on the oceanfront that has become established as an all-the-year attraction." The fishing pier, pictured on a c.1930s linen card, had a statewide following. (Courtesy of Kathi McGrath)

Since most mid-19th century steamers sailed into the South Shrewsbury River, or the river's "long branch," which becomes Branchport Creek, this stream was a locale of multiple docks. On arriving, an overland trip was still needed to reach the oceanfront hotels. Planning to build a substantial pier on the ocean became a long, thorny process. The *Times* recounted discussions on August 17, 1871, reflecting optimism that the substantial funds required could be raised if only the community could fix a location and type of pier. A pier would also afford an ancillary benefit, as it was claimed one could serve as a docking place in storms. The cautious were wary about what was wished for, observing that a "landing pier," or one that would permit vessels to arrive and depart the same day, would help lessen the Branch's exclusivity. This would encourage visitation by day-trippers, perhaps including riff-raff not unlike those who diminished nearby Coney Island and the Rockaways on Long Island. The wait continued, but in the interim, according to historical accounts, a flimsy wood pier

was erected in 1872, one that allegedly lasted about a week. Captain Isaac B. Smith, owner of the East Coast Hotel, built and paid for a pier of pine which endured for the 1875 season, but it succumbed to a furious September gale. Importantly, however, it demonstrated the practicality of an ocean pier that could dock large steamboats without damage to pier or vessel.

The selection of the pier's location was critical and difficult, because many hotel owners wished their frontage selected. The dissatisfaction of some following the selection of the Ocean House shore resulted in agitation for a second pier. Engineers studied piers worldwide in order to assure attaining the peak of technology and functionality. The Long Branch pier, engineered by Maclay and Davis of New York, was built of tubular iron and extended about 660 feet into the ocean to a point where the water was expected to be calm. The deck elevation was planned to be 19 ½ feet above low water and 15 feet above the high tide. Construction, which began in late 1878, was completed by June. The pier

The Haunted Mansion may have been the pier's all-time most popular attraction. Built as part of a major 1978 pier renovation, numerous character actors along with special lighting and sound effects created a bizarre funhouse. The Cinema 180 in the center was described as a bubble-like theatre-in-the-round. They are pictured on a c.1980 post card. (Courtesy of Kathi McGrath)

Significant change over an approximate 20-year span is reflected on a c.1960 post card and a c.1980 aerial photograph. The earlier dating is suggested by the presence of the stadium on the right. The later date is suggested by the pier reconstruction and the presence of the water slide, the small wavy lines in the center. A number of minor changes in the built environment can also be detected. Our Lady Star of the Sea, the tall structure visible in the center of the later image, is often a constant for comparative landscape viewing.

To appreciate the profound recent changes in the shorefront, compare this with the Pier Village picture on the chapter's last page where Star of the Sea is also visible. (Card – Courtesy of Kathi McGrath; Photograph – Courtesy of Historian, Fort Monmouth)

Long Branch, N. J.

docked its first ship, the *Adelaide,* on the 15th as her captain delicately maneuvered the vessel to enable it to be secured by the inexperienced pier hands. The pier immediately drew a wide public, both passengers and shore-side visitors. The latter willingly paid an admission to enjoy the appeal of walking over the water. However, problems accompanied the popular success. The pier was not of sufficient length to enable docking in adverse conditions, so it was lengthened the following winter. Then a storm wrecked the pier which required the building of a new one in 1881. Despite all, ocean steamer travel endured. Confusion exists over names of the two piers, "iron" and "ocean." Both were constructed of iron, although the 1881 wrought iron was a major improvement over the earlier tubular iron. "Ocean pier" was a generic term for a structure that extended sufficiently distant into the water to enable a vessel to land. A public following was built through a low fare and a ride that was appealing when conditions were right. However, bad weather could make the trip unreliable, while shipping lines probably had some unprofitable years, which is inferred by periodic changes of boats and questions in the press regarding which ships might be on the ocean run for the next season.

Long-term reliable transport to the Branch would be provided by the railroad. It was for practical purposes initially a hybrid with steamer travel on the Raritan and Delaware Bay, which began operation in June, 1860. The line's announcement as a road to southern Jersey was a subterfuge that was planned to break the Camden and Amboy's monopoly of New York to Philadelphia traffic, a story beyond the ambit of this work. A spur was built from the main Raritan and Delaware Bay track at Eatontown to Long Branch, which produced revenue as the line fought and lost a costly legal struggle with its powerful monopolistic opponent. Steamer travel from New York to an inhospitable pier at Shoal Harbor (renamed Port Monmouth) in Middletown Township, which was required before reaching the railroad cars, was neither easy nor reliable. However, this trip was an effective alternative to an even more difficult steamer run to Branchport Creek.

More effective rail transport preceded the iron pier by four years. It was provided by the New York and Long Branch Railroad, which was built by the Central Railroad of New Jersey and opened in 1875. While this was promoted as the "all land route," the claim was mildly hyperbolic, as New York passengers still needed to cross the Hudson via a short ferry trip to reach the rail terminal at Jersey City. The line was not only a conduit to the resorts – it transformed Long Branch. The road ran along Long Branch's length, and metaphorically paved the

way for development of its interior. While the tracks were laid only two blocks west of Ocean Avenue, the Long Branch stop befit its local informal name of the "central station." Travel to the Branch by rail and steam, which co-existed for decades, offered choices in reliability, glamour and price. Under ideal travel conditions, the ocean run was pleasant and enjoyable, an experience comparable to the high-speed ferry service popular in the early 21st century on the Raritan Bay to New York run. However, travel conditions were often less than ideal.

The ocean pier endured for over two decades, surviving problems such as repeated damage by storms (and ostensibly by a vessel in 1893), damage that was regularly repaired. The pier's demise was foretold by repeated buffeting by storms at the turn of the 20th century. The press reported the various extents of washed away sections and then in 1901 came the final blow, storm damage that rendered the pier unusable. The talk about rebuilding the pier went on for years, but it was the development of Ocean Park that finally turned the talk into action. Announcements were made to build a grand pier that would include an elaborate above-surface structure. However, in 1912, only a modest recreation pier was built, one that lacked docking capabilities. Direct steamer service to the ocean shore had reached its end.

The impact of the ocean steamer on Long Branch merits deeper study, but the conclusion is manifest. The numerous day-trippers brought by the boats popularized Long Branch, but at the not unexpected cost of loss of exclusivity. However, the pier's popularity served its owners well and provided an inexpensive travel alternative. This was revealed in a press exchange in November 1883 when it was reported that the pier would be sold to the Central Railroad, a transaction that hinged on price. The pier did not sell, in part because the pier owner was making a comfortable 10% return on investment. In addition, while denying the sale, the pier company's president also cited that their 60 cents fare benefited a public which otherwise might be required to pay $1.50 to the railroad. However, there are contemporary reports of financial hardship, so one may infer that the expense of repairs consumed any profits. Also realize that disparate economic needs of steamer operators and pier managers vs. the city created opposite goals. Any paying passenger brought revenue to the former, but the day-trippers gave minimal benefit to Long Branch. Similarly, the end of horse racing, posited elsewhere in this volume as a social boon to the city was a money-losing bane to the pier and vessel owners. The 1912 pier was consistent with resort counterparts as it provided a place to recreate and enjoy a variety of amusements and activities. The pier endeared itself to generations of visitors as a place for fun, thousands who had no idea of the pier's transport origins. The pier's changing mix of features is depicted in the vast number of images preserved over the decades. Sport fishing became a principal activity and gave rise to an informal nickname of "the fishing pier." Perhaps appreciation of the pier and its contribution to the history of recreation at the shore was fully recognized only after its destruction by fire on June 8, 1987.

The Shore Hotels

The Long Branch lodging industry originated with colonial era boarding houses, hostelries with few records or contemporary accounts. Some are known to have expanded into hotels. This 1860 list of the principal hotels and their capacities may be the earliest known detailed compilation:

Metropolitan, 500
National, 500
Congress/Hall, 150
Mansion House, 500
United States, 350
Pavilion, 350
Bath Hotel, 200
Howland House, 300
Conover House, 150
Alleghany, 250
St. Nicholas, 200
Ocean House, 150

One wonders how capacity was calculated or by whom because on busy weekends, folding cots could be placed nearly anywhere for the unexpected seekers of sleeping space. While early imagery is scant, the aforementioned Schenk creates an excellent insight into the industry in 1868. The pictures in his *Album* reveal a dreary row of typically three or four story boxes, lined-up along the shore in close proximity, forming their own conflagration zone. The northern section of the famed engraving "Long Branch from the Sea" from a sketch by Theodore R. Davis depicts that row. Published by *Harper's Weekly*, August 23, 1873, the example from Moss and Schnitzspahn reprinted in the introduction, is enhanced by its inserted labels with directional arrows.

The hotel that Henry Fernbach of New York designed for Alexander M. Cristalar, completed in 1862, is probably the end-gabled core that was enveloped by his 1863 expansion. When Joline Avenue (then Troutman) ran to Ocean Avenue, this hotel was on its northwest corner. Initially called the Atlantic Hotel, name changes included the Arlington House and the East End Hotel, its identity when damaged in an 1880 storm that closed the place prior to its demolition in 1881. John Hoey bought the property, but never carried out plans for a hotel. See The Reservation in Chapter 1, which traces Nate Salsbury's c.1900 purchase and his development. The hotel's site is now part of Seven Presidents Oceanfront Park.

The hotel's simple frame construction facilitated the expansion and growth that followed the signal year of 1860, when the railroad arrived. Owners that needed more rooms simply added a wing, until some structures nearly reached their neighbors. Revelation of their character could vary with the source consulted. The *Long Branch News*" (June 29, 1865) waxed enthusiastic with local boosterism when describing a place:

"Three stories high with four turrets rising from the roof. There are 250 chambers, 20 private parlors, and there are upwards of 40 miles of bell wire distributed though the house. There are gas and bells in every room. There are bathrooms, and every other convenience in every floor, that is to be found in the most fashionable hotels."

But Olive Logan in the *Harper New Monthly Magazine* of September 1876, grumbled:

It has been a newspaper fashion lately to call Long Branch the American Brighton, but a Brighton it certainly is not and will never be until the barn-like frame buildings which serve it as hotels are pulled down and others are erected of a material more solid, substantial and imposing. It is these sprawling wooden structures which give to Long Branch that cheap and tawdry air – the place is very suggestive of a circus.

The 1854 Metropolitan Hotel, built at the northwest corner of Ocean and Cooper Avenues, had undergone recent reconstruction by its new owner-partnership of Samuel Laird and Joseph H. Cooper when pictured by Schenck in 1868. The grounds were located a few yards from the East Long Branch station, the 1865 original terminus of the Long Branch and Seashore Railroad. When owned by Dr. Arthur V. Conover, (who had bought the extensive Wardell farm just north of Long Branch), and undergoing renovations, the Metropolitan was destroyed by fire on April 25, 1876. It had been described at the time as one of the largest and best-appointed shore hotels.

The Clarendon Hotel at the southwest corner of Ocean and North Broadway, built in 1835 by Hugh Manahan to replace the Lane's End Hotel, was owned by Dr. H.T. Hembold when published by Schenck. It had apparently faded not long after this 1868 illustration as the *Times* of August 10, 1875 reported, "The Clarendon has been turned into a good boarding house, such as they have at Saratoga, and this is a great gain." It was reported being sold and altered in 1882. The Clarendon was the Ocean Wave by 1889.

The Continental Hotel, the largest of the early hostelries, one that spanned a full block below South Broadway, or the current site of the Ocean Place (hotel), was an 1866 amalgam of a new center section with older hotels connected on the north, the National, and Congress Hall on the south. It was then-owned by Long Branch real estate magnate Woolman Stokes, but attained greater renown following the 1872 acquisition by the Lelands, among America's finest hotel operators. Pictured here from Schenck, they renamed it the Ocean Hotel.

These oversized, dull shabby structures endured despite Logan's protestations. That 1876 date may have been their high point. It was the final year of Grant's second term, the one President who spent appreciable time at the Branch. Monmouth Park racing was in its seventh season, while the big city high rollers enjoyed club-life, a euphemism for Long Branch's special appeal, gambling. Actually, as with the clubs, what went on inside made the places special. The dining, the dancing, and the entertainments gave rise to their collective sobriquet "the grand hotels." The press of the day reported hotel arrivals as news. Clientele ranged from the era's social blue bloods to ethnic groups, each clustering at a favored hotel. However, socializing could conceal the pedigree of the merrymakers. The balls, hops and other events embraced broad swaths of citizenry which could leave a lady uncertain if her attentions drew a ranking gentleman or a modest boarder from an inland rooming house.

Hotels were typically income properties where ownership and operation were generally in different hands. Managers switched hotels and, at times, an owner might have been forced to operate his own place after losing a manager. The players changed, while the system worked, endured, and prospered. Prosperity probably produced a complacency that precluded reinvestment As a consequence, the Long Branch hotel stock was permitted to age and deteriorate. Was there a "greatest blow?" The resort industry was long subject to both the vagaries of the economy and local circumstances. Two local events are often, but incorrectly, cited as causes of the decline. Actually, neither the 1893 cessation of horse racing (in a depression year), nor the 1905 enforcement of anti-gambling laws had a significant effect, historical accounts to the contrary notwithstanding. Decrepit old hotels were falling or burning at the close of the 19th century. Lack of investment was the greatest problem with the industry then. Their demise coincided with, or perhaps even prompted, the independence of the City of Long Branch. This change of governance prompted an oceanfront renewal and a change of the city's character for the new century. The core of this subject, introduced here, demands deeper study because it is at the crux of Long Branch history.

The long row of shorefront hotels is captured by this engraving from the 19th century illustrated press, undated, but after the 1872 renaming to the Ocean Hotel. Note the still-considerable bluff, not yet worn-away by the elements, and the "Saratoga Water" stand, located near the stairs. The pier was built at this point in 1879, which helped the place "improve" sanitation, at least by the standards of the day. The pier permitted the Ocean Hotel to dump waste at sea from the pier instead of into cesspools.

The Cooper Cottage, here amidst the hotels, represents the origin of Long Branch lodging as the boarding house. Schenck notes its core dates from Robert Parker's c.1816 farmhouse, which was expanded by Samuel Cooper in mid-century. The place, located behind Ocean Avenue near the former New Jersey Southern station, was known as the Irving House when destroyed by fire in July 1881. (Schenck)

The Pavilion Hotel, although one of Long Branch's oldest, was omitted from Schenck's *Album*, but his *Descriptive Guide* listed it as one of the Branch's eight "respectable" hotels. Built in 1851 and conducted by Gouveneur S.C. Morris of New York who resided here year-round with his family, the *Times* reported on August 17, 1859 that the Pavilion was "famous for large rooms and apparently under the especial patronage of the children of Israel." A side street, Pavilion Avenue, was opened later and named for the hotel. Renamed the Atlantic at an unspecified date, Pavilion was restored briefly at the turn of the 20th century, but it was soon the Atlantic again. The Atlantic was destroyed by fire on August 16, 1925, a tragic blaze that killed two firemen and one employee. The New Atlantic Hotel was built on the site.

Schenck declared that the Mansion House on Ocean Avenue north of Chelsea Avenue originated in 1846 as the Morris House, while Samuel Laird added the south wing (left) and renamed the place after his 1852 purchase. When devastated by an incendiary fire on December 20, 1884, the *Times* reported the next day that the main building was completely destroyed, but the wing was saved. The Mansion House was rebuilt, but details of its last years are scant. The *Times,* again, on June 2, 1912, indicated that the penultimate of the old ocean hotels "has vanished. The building …was recently sold, cut in two and moved to a point on Chelsea Avenue."

In 1868 Samuel Laird also acquired the United States Hotel off the southwest corner of Ocean and Chelsea, which he operated in conjunction with the Mansion House north of Chelsea. The place, which was built in 1852 by F. Kennedy in association with George and Isaac Crater, occupied a 13 acre tract that ran west to the railroad. The hotel operated into the early 20th century, but the *Times* reported June 28, 1903 that it had been torn down. Pier Village fills both the United States Hotel and Mansion House sites. Compare with the picture at the chapter's end, in which a prominent Chelsea Avenue points the viewer to the area. (Schenck)

The Hotel Pannaci was built by Patrick McCormick, but the place's first historical record was as Iauch's Hotel for Anthony who bought it in 1868. Located on Ocean Avenue about 150 feet north of North Bath Avenue, the c.1912 post card reflects its new name following the 1899 purchase by Gernando Pannaci. The hotel was known during each of these incarnations for its fine cuisine. Countering a trend to the north, Pannaci prospered into the 20th century, having been expanded and improved twice in its first decade, but could not survive the Depression. The Pannaci closed and was demolished in 1932. (Courtesy of John Rhody)

The Howland House originated c.1828 as Obadiah Sayrs' Sayrs House, but Henry Howland had been owner for 24 years when pictured by Schenck. He noted that the place long-had a Philadelphia clientele, which the *Times* of May 3, 1873 reinforced by calling the Howland, "a favorite stopping place for staid and quiet Philadelphians." The Howland was expanded several times, but declined by century's end. Following the auctioning of its contents in 1906, the Howland deteriorated. After unsuccessful attempts to condemn the once grand place, the Howland was described in June 1912 as an eyesore tottering in the breeze, prior to destruction by fire that December 11. Howland Avenue later split the hotel's site which is now filled with apartments and townhouses.

The Scarboro Hotel, designed by John M. Merrick of New York, was described when built in 1882 as an ornate Queen Anne building, which suggests that this c.1910 post card reflects an early remodeling. The short 60 foot end faced Ocean Avenue, while the 200 feet of frontage that was on South Bath Avenue is pictured at the right.

Louis Shapiro, who purchased the Scarboro around 1915, remodeled the hotel and expanded it along the ocean side. The Scarboro advertised itself as "catering only to a select patronage" and offered private baths in each room before that was the standard. The undated, perhaps c.1930 photograph, depicts the carefully kept grounds and impressive façade that conveyed the Scarboro's luxury. The place was destroyed by fire on September 12, 1941.

The Hotel Takanassee, built in 1906 on the site of the West End Hotel, (Chapter 3) was the new century's first new promise for resurrection of its hotel stock. While it was for two decades the only new hope in Long Branch, the appealing place failed in the Great Depression, demolished at an unspecified date, reportedly to save taxes. A 1907 press account referenced a chief architect Wilson, although he has not been identified. The dining room had been on the fifth floor, but around the time of this c.1910 Underwood photographic post card, that space had been converted to an amusement area/ballroom, while first floor dining facilities included a room erected on the lawn east of the hotel. The Diplomat Apartments were later on the site. (Courtesy of John Rhody)

P630   Hotel Takanassee, West End, N. J.

HOTEL VENDOME, LONG BRANCH, N. J.

Durnell claims that John Daly's Long Branch Club was remodeled to the Hotel Vendome after gambling closed. The dome is a recognizable point of comparison, but the basic structure was expanded beyond recognition. The Vendome, which faced the ocean on the block between South Bath Avenue and Cottage Place, was strictly kosher and managed by Mrs. H. Schneider & Son at the time of this c.1920s post card. Their promotional slogan rhymed: "Make the Vendome your Summer Home." The time of its demise is not specified. (Courtesy of Glenn Vogel)

The Fountains Motel was built in 1958 at 160 Ocean Avenue on the northwest corner of Morris. The house with the bell-shaped tower was the Jefferson Park Parish Fresh Air Home. The place became firmly and fondly fixed in public cognizance during its less than half-century existence, even being called a "landmark" at its October 2005 auction of contents preparatory to demolition. The site remains vacant at the end of 2008. (Courtesy Long Branch Public Library)

When Hilton opened its hotel and convention center in 1990, Long Branch was not part of the name, the chain choosing the ambiguous "Ocean Place." That name has endured through a number of owners, although the form is now Ocean Place Resort and Spa. The hotel, designed by William B. Tabler, Architects, of New York, which contains a 10,000 square foot exhibition hall and a 1,000 seat ballroom, was its era's greatest hope for business growth and development in Long Branch, but it appeared so alone for two decades. Holding the address One Ocean Boulevard, the hotel is located directly east of South Broadway at the shore where its construction cut-off Ocean Avenue. The 2008 photograph looks at the long south and short east elevations.

The definitive origins of the Hotel Riviera may be lost in obscurity, but the building perhaps dates from the 1920s. The place was advertised in the 1940s under Fred Lizza's ownership as Long Branch's "leading Italian American hotel." The then unoccupied hotel and an adjacent rooming house on the corner of Morris Avenue were destroyed by fire on November 9, 1956. Stef's Court Motel was built on the site in 1959. (Courtesy of John Rhody)

Amedeo and Antoinette Stefanelli opened this motel in 1959, known as Stef's Court, on the site of the destroyed Riviera. Reflecting a change in accommodations, they offered "new modern efficiencies and seasonal rates." The façade faces Morris Avenue on the north, while a glimpse of the boardwalk is on the left edge. Still standing in 2008, it is now known as the Ocean Court Motel, not to be confused with the Ocean Place, the two sharing a word that can hardly be trademarked.

The Casino and Ocean Park

Soon after cutting ties with Ocean Township, local officials were confronted with a dilapidated city, its resort industry decimated, the elements buffeting both the bluff and Ocean Avenue, its greatest physical asset, while the draw of gambling, however dismal the crowd it brought, disappeared. Long Branch then opted to appeal to families. An attractive spot became available, the site of the former Ocean Hotel, which was already home to a small frame recreational casino, one of many structures moved to the New Jersey shore after the 1876 Philadelphia Centennial Exposition closed. Then local government, invigorated by the 1904 reaffirmation of independent city status and determined to remake the fading town, spent heavily and assumed substantial debt for the construction of Ocean Park and its new casino. While the new facility remade a section of shore at public expense, the expected private parallel investment did not follow.

This September 1911 post card view is dated by its *New York Times* publication on the 11th under a headline, "New Pier At Long Branch Nearing Completion." The *Times* image depicted construction equipment at the end of the pier, which the post card publisher deleted. Samuel R. Rosoff was constructing a costly $1.5 million concrete pier and the new Ocean Amusement Park, which, judging by the picture, appeared to be open already. (Courtesy Rutgers Special Collections and University Archives)

This early 20th century photograph is older than the companion image, as the building became the annex after the large casino was completed. Note the painted Coca-Cola sign on a South Broadway building. (Courtesy of Karen L. Schnitzspahn)

This photograph of the casino's east façade was taken late in its career. Dating is provided by the "Jimmy Maloney" sign. This heavyweight contender worked-out here in early 1927 preparatory to a bout with underdog Jack Sharkey, who, giving a 10-pound advantage to Bostonian Maloney, beat the stuffing out of him in April at Yankee Stadium. The place was destroyed by fire the next year.

Note the roof balustrade, perhaps erected as the new casino was completed. The image is a c.1910 post card. (Courtesy of John Rhody)

1410   Ocean Park, Long Branch, N. J.

Ground was broken for the new casino in June 1906 after litigation over the site caused a year's delay. It opened a year later. The southerly view on this c.1912 post card taken from South Broadway shows the relationship among the several structures. The amusement park was described with puffery in the *Times* of April 28, 1912 with a claim it was to be made a sort of Dreamland (the fantastic Coney Island Park). Actually, there was no comparison.

This ad from the June 28, 1911 *Red Bank Register* describes a few features and indicates pier builder Rosoff's remaining for a managerial role.

The framing behind the old casino's bandstand appears to be for the 1907 casino, which would date this photographic post card. The bandstand crowd seems packed, if not filling every inch. Apparently quite a crowd could jam the place if the July 7, 1907 account in the *Times* is accurate, they claiming that "not less than 40,000 attended 4th of July celebrations at Ocean Park."

The Scenic Railway, an early name for roller coaster, was developed by L.A. Thompson and first built in Coney Island's Luna Park in the 1890s. Present at the 1911 opening of Ocean Park, William Piper's Long Branch Scenic Railway may be better known for its tragic end. His son Raymond, while operating a car on August 31, 1913, lost his hold while on a curve at its highest point and fell 85 feet to his death. A passenger guided the car to its destination, but the coaster operation ceased then, was dismantled and moved. The rails had been located directly behind the footprint of the future new casino. (Courtesy of John Rhody)

A circus by the sea is pictured on an undated post card, perhaps c.1911. (Courtesy of Glenn Vogel)

Long Branch Stadium

The city, suffering from the Depression and desperate to raise revenue, concocted a plan that embraced what we now regard as barbaric abuse of animals. Some thought that greyhound racing would skirt the state's ban on pari-mutual betting through a technicality and, emboldened with a legislative act to permit dog tracks in debt-burdened municipalities, the city built Long Branch Stadium in 1934 for a reported $150,000. Facing the ocean between South Broadway and Laird Street, the stadium became the venue for the gambling-powered, cruel and crude exhibition of dog racing. Some in Long Branch favored the measure as a stimulus to business activity. The greedy, eager backers thought the state constitution would countenance this gambling because the 1874 amendment barred the "use of gambling devices now in use", while new pari-mutual betting techniques had since been developed. The Long Branch Kennel Club, headed by Mayor Goldberg, began racing in July. The dogs chased a mechanical rabbit, typically for 27 seconds over a quarter-mile. Betting, which was challenged in court, was ruled unconstitutional in late September. The finding was also an impediment to equine interests who viewed the canine event as a prelude to resumption of horse racing with pari-mutual betting, an effort that came to fruition in the post-World War II period. The dog interests tried again in 1936, attempting to use an "option system" of wagering similar to one employed in Nassau County, New York as a way around the betting ban. The artifice failed, while state police guarded the place to prevent gambling. After 16 days of racing, the place closed August 24th.

Greyhound Racing

TEN RACES NIGHTLY

EXCEPT SUNDAYS

RAIN OR SHINE   NO MINORS

For Box Reservations Call Long Branch 124

After 2 P. M.

●

ADMISSION INCLUDING TAX

Club House $1.25   Grandstand 50c

Long Branch Kennel Club

Ocean Avenue, Long Branch

The organizational name in this August 4, 1934 advertisement from *The Stroller,* "kennel club" might lead one to believe they promoted the care of animals rather than engage in their mistreatment.

Midget automobile racing followed the dogs, succeeded by stock cars in the post-World War II era. The dirty, noisy operation was a blight. Pictured on a c.1950 linen post card, the stadium was demolished at an unspecified date, perhaps c.1960. (Courtesy of John Rhody)

OCEAN BOULEVARD AND BEACH, LOOKING NORTH, LONG BRANCH, N. J.

The absence of readily visible dating aids leads one to project this linen post card as 1940s.

July 26, 1866 was a feel-good day for the New Jersey Militia. They had been enjoying their annual encampment at Long Branch, were admired by many of the seaside visitors and the governor was coming for a review. The front of the Continental Hotel was the chosen site and while the 3:00 PM scheduled start was delayed, Governor Marcus L. Ward, General Runyon and their respective staffs rode up and down the line for a satisfying inspection of the troops. The Frank Leslie artist captured the throng, a veritable sea of humanity.

REVIEW OF THE NEW JERSEY STATE MILITIA BY GOVERNOR WARD AT LONG BRANCH, JULY 26, 1866.—[SKETCHED BY STANLEY FOX.]

The original image is labeled "Central Block," a row of stores on the southwest corner of Ocean and Chelsea Avenues, adjacent to the Central Hotel. Cranmer's Baths was later built on the site, which was cleared for the occupancy there at publication, Pier Village, this part on its eastern edge.

The breeze was blowing both the bathing hour's white flag and the skirts of these on-lookers on the 1869 day of Winslow Homer's (1836-1910) iconic shore painting, *Long Branch, New Jersey.* Since 1941 the 16 by 21 ¾-inch oil has been in the collection of the Museum of Fine Arts, Boston, the artist's place of birth. The parasols were hardly decorative as many visitors feared the surf for harm to the complexion and it was still believed that bathing was a little risqué at best, or simply vulgar. The bluffs above, not to be overlooked, were eloquently described by *Harper's Weekly* August 24, 1867, they, "instead of being covered by the white sand glaring in the sunshine, are carpeted by a green sward, pleasant to the eye."

In Winslow Homer's well-know print, *On the Bluff at Long Branch, at the Bathing Hour,* published by *Harper's Weekly,* August 6, 1871, the white flag signifying the bathing hour is flying. Lore claims that red and white flags signaled beach time for men and women respectively, but by 1866 Schenck (*Descriptive Guide*) informs that the white flag was "the bathing hour" for all, men then having exclusive use of the beach until 6:00AM for the "privilege of disporting in natural abandon." These well-wrapped maids descending towards the Bathing Dresses shed remind the reader how infrequently the outline of the female form, or their skin, was seen in the Victorian-era. Relishing the female form inspired one writer to wax enthusiastic in the *Times* of August 15, 1865, "I assert boldly that a lady who is arrayed in a neat and tasty bathing-dress is never more attractive than at that particular moment…a lady is beautiful when she once gets into the surf and the garments cling to the graceful form." What would he have thought in 2008, especially when there is so often so little to cling?

The amusements in post-Civil War Long Branch would hardly engage the resort visitor of the early 21st century. As an 1866 correspondent observed, "A walk on the beach, a bath and a drive seem to while the hours away." While the trip to the Branch was a modest fare, the cost of hired carriages could drive-up the stay's expense. A few years later another wrote of the late afternoon coming alive, of dust-controlled, sprinkled Ocean Avenue, that it "gets to be worth looking at. Its animated show of horses, vehicles and riders is a contrast with the previous drowsiness…Many of the teams are noticeably handsome and some of the horses are fast trotters." (Granville Perkins' print, *The Drive* first appeared in *Appleton's Journal*, September 7, 1872.

Philadelphian Richard J. Dobbins, one of Long Branch's major real estate developers, built Spray Cottage around the 1870s adjacent to the Howland Hotel, pictured at the left, which he held for rental. (Courtesy Long Branch Public Library)

The "Baby Parade" was a "pageant" for young girls to show off their well-dressed dolls in an array of carts, barrows and carriages. While the first parade in August 1907 was described as having an inland route beginning on Broadway, this post card from a few years later points out the event had become annual and the route moved to Ocean Avenue. (Courtesy of Glenn Vogel)

The noted architect Edward T. Potter of New York designed the simple, unornamented lines of Henry M. Alexander's Beach Drive house. It was completed around 1859, preceding the rapidly surrounding development. Its nickname, *The Grove,* is ironical in the absence of trees, but reminiscent of modern developments, embracing "Heights", for example, the flatness of their surroundings notwithstanding. Actually, mid-19th century Long Branch was esteemed for the wooded area so close to the shore, but the barrenness of the beachfront properties were a recognized tradeoff for proximity to the water. (Schenck)

Cranmer's pool near the southwest corner of Chelsea and Ocean Avenues is pictured c.1910 prior to a major expansion. The c.1870s Second Empire style houses on the north side of Chelsea reflect its one-time residential character. A glimpse of the old Star of the Sea Church is in the background.

The waterslide, located on the west side of Ocean Avenue, is pictured in July 1978, when planned as one of the feature attractions of the new pier organization. It was not the only way to get wet there; the adjacent Bumper Boat ride consisted of little craft that looked like tubes with seats.

Chelsea Bath's enormous pool at the northwest corner of Chelsea and Ocean Avenues was laid out perpendicular to Chelsea, while the stores at top right faced Ocean. Contributing to scant historical details is a 1930 news account indicating that this pool was being expanded. The year was about the end of the white border post card era. While its destruction date is not recorded, the north front section of Pier Village is on the site now.

The faux jungle in the midst of Broadway miniature golf, which soon disappeared, gave this early 1980s chrome postcard a dated look.

A view of Ocean Avenue looking north in 1979 is a reminder of the city's palm tree beautification effort. They lent a visual appeal, but the New Jersey climate was not propitious to their survival. They did not. The site, looking towards Broadway, was on the miniature golf course adjacent to the boardwalk. Note the 28- by 16-foot granite enclosure at the Garfield statue's original location, barely visible on the left.

While an unoccupied beach might suggest an off-season image, in this instance the empty chair reflects a summer closure for health safety concerns in the 1980s.

Cranmer's on the southwest corner of Chelsea is behind the pole on the left. The pier is right of center while boardwalk business sprouted up by the time of this c.1940 linen post card. (Courtesy of Glenn Vogel)

Two views about ten years apart show change on Ocean Avenue looking north from above Chelsea. The carnival scene – there may be a parade in progress – is about 1912. Straw hats are few, but one made it to the beach. (Courtesy of John Rhody)

In 1929, (a few years prior to this photograph) the Ocean Pier Amusement Company bought for a reported $500,000 the New Arcade, a structure with 34 stores that fronted 500 feet on the boardwalk near Chelsea Avenue (*Times* April 19, 1929) (Courtesy of Karen L. Schnitzspahn)

The crowd is overdressed by later standards, but one knows this is a summer scene from the men's straw hats which by then were de rigueur. By the time of this 1920s white border post card, the median had been built and new street lights erected. (Courtesy of Kathi McGrath)

This c.1960 chrome post card view, which looks north from Morris Avenue, depicts the 1958 Fountains Motel on the north side of that street. The blue spot under the base of the pier is the massive Chelsea Baths pool. Cranmer's is obscured by its L-shaped enclosure on the south side of Chelsea opposite Chelsea Baths. (Courtesy of John Rhody)

The National Guard Armory was completed in 1959 at the northwest corner of Ocean and Cooper Avenues on the site of the former Hotel Avenel. While home to the 250th Supply and Transportation Battalion, the building's career included housing a youth counseling organization, various exhibitions and even a 1970 Bruce Springsteen concert. After a protracted period of vacancy during city ownership and following a contentious issue over sale to a developer, the armory was demolished around January 2000 for the construction of a private health club.

The seven-foot Garfield memorial sculpted by Swiss-born, European-trained Philadelphia artist J. Otto Schweizer originally stood in Ocean Park, on Ocean Avenue, where a reported crowd of 25,000 witnessed a parade and ceremony for its September 2, 1918 dedication. The event culminated the 12-year efforts of the Garfield Memorial Association to erect a suitable memorial to the president who had died in Long Branch in 1881. At the ceremony, Governor Walter E. Edge, citing Garfield's support of labor, celebrated workers for their contribution to the raging war then in its final months. The statue is pictured in 2008 at Presidential Park in front of the Ocean Place Resort and Spa; is was moved there around 1990. The park, which was commissioned by the Long Branch Historical Association and dedicated in July 1997, has bronze plaques honoring the seven presidents associated with Long Branch. The statue needs preservation, the accumulation of foreign matter in its green patina reducing the definition of the figure's details.

Scott Towers, later Seaview Towers, at 390-2 Ocean Avenue exemplifies the short useful life of construction of the second half of the 20th century and the value of waterfront property in a rising market. Demolition of the seven-story apartments, built in 1955 without air-conditioning, has been planned since 2003 for replacement with eight-story condominiums. Pictured in July 2008, one wonders about the near-term fate of this site, formerly occupied by the Scarboro Hotel, as the book is completed late in the year. The period's economic doldrums has left the market for luxury construction anywhere but rising.

Apartments and condominiums line the shore once dotted with hotels. The Sea Verge at 385 Ocean Avenue, an appealing example from the recent past, is pictured in 2008. Look! Even absent an ocean exposure, one can soak-up afternoon rays on the west-facing balconies. The Versailles was likely the last hotel at the south side of the South Bath Avenue site.

A gale along the shore made Monmouth lifesavers wary early on November 15, 1906. The *Samuel C. Holmes,* built 1880 in Milford Delaware, was carrying pine lumber from Queen Anne Court House, Virginia to New York when the 95-foot, 79-ton, three-masted schooner was blown around by the high winds. With its sails shredded and carried away, Capt. John J. Evans' only course was to try to beach the helpless vessel. He and a crew of three were rescued in a breeches buoy. It had been a busy day for the lifesavers, this ship having been preceded by the wreck of the two-masted *James M. Hall.* The photographic post card was the news of the early 20th century. Do not wonder if the vessel was re-floated; the surf pounded it to pieces the next day.

Ill-fate plagued the *New Era* even before reaching Long Branch waters. The 1,240-ton packet built in Maine and launched in April 1854, which sailed from Bremen September 19, 1854, lost three at sea in a storm, while cholera claimed another 40. The damaged ship ran aground in November near Life Saving Station No. 3 after being blown off course. The line secured for a lifesaving car broke, turning the rescue effort into a disaster, which took a toll of 240 of the 372 believed aboard. While no picture of the vessel exists, its image is familiar from an often-reproduced artist's impression painted the morning of the disaster. This substantial monument stands in the Old First Methodist Church cemetery in West Long Branch.

A large engraving of this beached wreck labeled the *Dora Baker* was published by *Harper's Weekly* on August 24, 1867. Do not mistake it for a major maritime disaster as the paper briefly described this sketch, made from in front of the Stetson House (later West End), as "the wreck of a small vessel, probably a schooner named the *Dora Baker*, which went ashore there last spring." Schenck's *Descriptive Guide* tells that "Portions of wrecks are often thrown up on the beach, and becoming imbedded in the sand, remain as fixtures for months, or even years, their jagged projections affording resting places for the stroller."

The steamer *St. Paul*, an impressive vessel that ran around January 24, 1896, was Long Branch's celebrated stranding. Until it became unstuck on February 4, the *St. Paul* was not only a rare winter tourist attraction, but was reportedly the biggest draw that Long Branch had had for some while. Excursion trains drew thousands from New York and Philadelphia. Visitors from the latter took special interest because the vessel was built there.

Monmouth Medical Center, the large building in the middle, is the focal of a 1961 aerial. Their original building that faced Third Avenue had been replaced earlier, while a Y-shaped series of structures face the viewer. The Borden Memorial Pavilion is on the south, or left, while the 1951 addition, then known as the Community Wing, is on the north. Over the decades, the facility has taken the remainder of the block east to Second Avenue, either for additional construction or parking. The short-lived, two-story brick railroad station is the light structure over the hospital. North Bath Avenue, the diagonal on the left, is marked by the then-new Adventurer Motel. Two lots to the north on Ocean Avenue the site of the former Iauch/Pannaci Hotel is vacant, but many of the old oceanfront houses still stood. The diagonal streets on the right are Pavilion, running to the hospital, and Morris Avenue, west of it. (Dorn's Classic Images)

There is hardly anything discernable in this 1960s aerial which is not visible on companion views, but the post card is in color and provides a long northerly perspective along the shore. The Fountains Motel at Morris Avenue is on the bottom, while the outline of the former stadium track is left of the pier. The largest of the gas holders, formerly standing north of lower Broadway, is also prominent. (Courtesy of John Rhody)

Pier Village, the focal and high point of the city's shore redevelopment area "is an established premier destination brimming with year-round activity" noted Greg Russo, an Applied Development Co. vice president. His firm and Pier Village architect Dean Marchetto have combined for numerous vital, aesthetically appealing projects in their base city of Hoboken. The ability of Pier Village to attract appealing retail and command significant rentals for the apartments over the stores has raised the bar for shorefront building. (Courtesy of Dean Marchetto)

The Constitution's Fifth Amendment states, "nor shall private property be taken for public use, without just compensation", specific protection against the recognized power of sovereign states of eminent domain. Most citizens believe that this power, which has been exercised since the nation's beginnings, was used for purposes benefiting the common good, notably public buildings or infrastructure projects, or, perhaps, slum clearance. However, in recent decades some jurisdictions interpreted "public use" broadly, defining it in the manner of Lewis Carroll's Humpty Dumpty, who in *Through the Looking Glass* declared, "When I use a word, it means just what I choose it to mean, neither more nor less." "Public use" at times was interpreted to include gentrification projects, removal of sound structures that some deemed were no-longer fitting in areas undergoing improvement. In some instances municipal figures saw the opportunity to create new attractive tax ratables by taking property at distressed "just" prices and turning it over to private developers who then benefited from the subsequent improvements. Many perceive these practices as "eminent domain abuse." The issue, which had been regularly litigated, reached the United States Supreme Court in a notable New London Connecticut case. In Long Branch, the use of eminent domain attained public outcry in a sound neighborhood of varying aesthetic appeal, which in most places would have been regarded as a close-knit haven by the sea. However, here it stood in the way of completing the Beachfront North redevelopment project. Homeowners' objections resulted in protracted litigation and a battle for public opinion.

Fears of mounting abuse stemmed from the Supreme Court's decision in favor of the City of New London, although not long after it some justices questioned the scope of the decision. In New Jersey, the appellate court established a standard for "blight" needed to justify taking by eminent domain. The small neighborhood, known as the MTOTSEA area for the streets of Marine Terrace, Ocean Terrace and Seaview Avenue did not meet this standard. The city was stymied; the homeowners won that phase. As this book is completed in late 2008, it appears that appeals will not test the ruling and the city will drop its efforts to condemn. While the Long Branch experience appears to be a major victory for property rights advocates in New Jersey, remaining uncertainty may not mean the case is concluded. The 2008 image looks west on Seaview Avenue from near the corner of Ocean Avenue.

Chapter 3.
Southern Neighborhoods
Elberon and West End

Elberon

The ill-wind that blew the riff-raff onto the ocean pier also blew a world of good to Long Branch's southern stem. That social change helped make Elberon an exclusive residential district. While artful cottages dotted the Elberon landscape prior to 1870, they were modest compared to the mansions that later established Elberon's elegance. Elberon was coined from the section's developer, Lewis B. Brown, a linkage more easily perceived when pronouncing his name using initials, as L.B. Brown. However, the name of the Central Railroad station of Elberon preceded the neighborhood, and since place-naming nomenclature steps back only one reference the neighborhood was technically named for the station, a minor, but real, distinction.

Lewis B. Brown had an early, but undeveloped, plan for an appealing reshaping of the ground. Blythe Beach Park, designed by the famed landscape architects Olmstead and Vaux, was mapped in 1867 and laid out in curvilinear streets that appealed to carriage travelers. However, the plan was effaced during subsequent development and the streets were reconfigured on a grid, leaving the artistic plan of Blythe Beach Park a memory.

This chapter presents a modest sampling of the mansions that made the splendor of Elberon, a section that runs from Takanasee Lake to the southern border. Despite loss of most of the mansions and profound change, Elberon's cachet remains strong, suggested by Elberon residents denoting their hometown as "Elberon," not Long Branch.

West End

The West End name has an obscure origin. West End, the section north of Elberon, marked the southerly end of the resort hotel district. The author recalls a 19th century map of Long Branch, one oriented with the west rather than the traditional north positioned at the top. Thus, the southern section of the city was on the left, or the customary place for the west. Ergo, "west end." While there is no corresponding "east end" in Long Branch, the northernmost of the shore hostelries, the East End Hotel, provides reinforcement for this geographic anomaly.

West End's stature, which pre-dated Elberon's, arose from its substantial houses, as home of the fine West End Hotel, and as the locale of John Hoey's fabulous Hollywood estate. Hollywood was begun as a private retreat, but Hoey attracted many visitors to his extensive, artistic grounds and was inspired to build many guest cottages and open a hotel, which became the city's finest. While West End's grandeur is gone and a modest business district bisects the neighborhood, West End also retains cachet and expects one to know it. As evidence, a present colleague of the author, when new to the area and doing consumer survey work, was given an address of West End. Her innocent inquiry regarding "the west end of what?" was met with icy, righteous indignation.

The railroad and post office reinforced community identity. The no-longer extant West End/Hollywood station once linked New York, Long Branch, and the Central railroad's Southern Division, but Elberon remains a station on the New York and Long Branch railroad. The post offices that were opened in both communities in 1881 remain as branches of the Long Branch office.

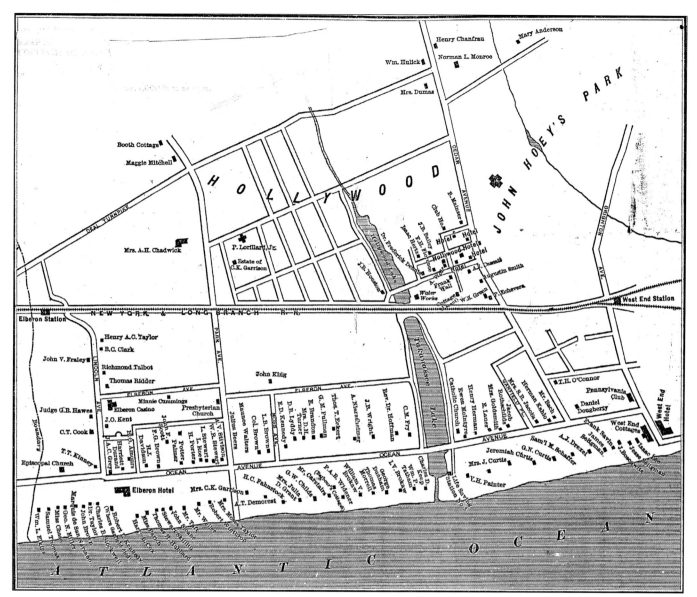

"Rich Elberon," the title of the August 16, 1886 *New York Herald* article in which this map first appeared, is a bluntly candid headline to denote the movement of the wealthy Long Branch crowd to that part of the city. The map clearly depicts most of the significant places described in this chapter. Note how the West End Hotel and Cottages faced Brighton Avenue in a short stem that linked Ocean Avenue's slight shift to the west. The map shows how the West End station served both the New York and Long Branch and the Central's Southern Division. Hoey's Hollywood was on both sides of Cedar, the cross north of it marking his home, while its public buildings were south of Cedar. Deal Turnpike at top, today's Norwood Avenue or Highway 71, marked Long Branch's western border. The Franklyn Cottage, regarded as a shrine, is parenthetically labeled "Where Garfield Died," while President Grant, who had also passed away, has his cottage labeled for his widow, "Mrs. Julia D. Grant." At the far left, the "Episcopal Church" would later be the famed Church of the Presidents, while the Presbyterian Church on Park is the Elberon Memorial. This book permits a small sampling of the houses. Some owners are changed, but the number of mapped structures depicts how well-populated this section had become.

This 1899 panorama of the West End Hotel shows the relationship between the hotel proper, center, and its cottages, the massive structure at the right. The loosely used term "cottage" in hotel parlance was typically any appendage that did not have dining facilities; cottage guests ate in the hotel's dining hall. The two are separated by Brighton Avenue, which met Ocean Avenue here with a sharp right-angled turn. The latter is spanned by the bridge leading to the pavilion on the beach. An 1876 account noted this hotel attracted a mix of New York, Philadelphia and Baltimore visitors helping make West End lively and fashionable. The cottages were destroyed by fire in February 1914.

The 1868 Schenck image of the Stetson House, once on the northwest corner of Ocean and Brighton Avenues, was a recent reconstruction and expansion of the Conover House, located on a plot that had been home to a hotel since Cornelius Lane's 1832 Lawn House. Built on an L-plan, the place shares the big box image of its northerly shore counterparts with one distinction, the absence of above grade "galleries" (porches) to assure privacy. Presbury and Hildreth bought the hotel in 1873, enlarged and improved it, renamed it the West End and earned a reputation as among Long Branch's best hotel operators.

Hildreth's bridge, pictured on a c.1905 Tuck post card, was described in 1888, presumably when new, as running 250 feet from the second story of the West End Hotel to a 2-story pavilion 40 feet above the surface. About 30 by 115 feet, it was an ideal resting place for water watching and breeze catching. The cottages had been regarded similarly; a visitor quoted in the June 30, 1873 *Times* claimed: "Its piazzas form one of the pleasantest meeting places to be found anywhere on the continent."

When opened in 1880, the *Times* indicated on May 30 that "Although this is called a row of cottages, its appearance is that of a large new hotel and it is one of the most elegantly appointed on the Atlantic coast." Each cottage contained 15 rooms, while each room faced either ocean or avenue. The complex, designed by Arthur Gilman of Long Branch, is pictured on a c.1910 post card. (Courtesy of Keith Wells)

John Chamberlain, a New York gambling operator, helped bring gaming to Long Branch after observing that his New York customers preferred the shore in the summer. John B. Terhune designed this appealing Second Empire style clubhouse and built it near the southwest corner of Ocean and Brighton Avenues. Completed in the spring of 1868 in time for the *Album of Long Branch* wherein Schenck claimed that Chamberlain is "to conduct this in a first class manner for the purposes of a club house." He did, but Schenck was likely unaware he was foretelling the impetus to the peak of Long Branch's popularity, but also the practice that would lead to the city's late-century decline. Not all would be surprised at the downward spiral. The *Times* was prescient on May 17, 1870, claiming when making reference to the new gambling house and racetrack, "It is doubtful whether they will contribute much to its (Long Branch) comfort or respectability."

Philadelphian Philip Daly took over Chamberlain's operation around 1876 with the backing of Richard J. Dobbins, expanded the facilities by erecting the domed structures at the right and renamed it the Pennsylvania Club. Daly, who attained stature among gambling operators for his integrity, lived by his motto, "a square deal" and was trusted implicitly by his elite and upper class customers. As a consequence of never fully recovering from a gunshot wound inflicted in 1888 by a robber in New York, Daly left active management to his son, Philip, Jr. The elder Daly survived nine years after gambling ended in 1901. The Wellington Inn occupant on the c.1907 post card reflects a short-term restaurant operation, as substantial demolition began in 1909. The site is now West End Park. (Courtesy of Glenn Vogel)

The origins of the early West End Casino are obscure. Early-on it was obviously a roller skating rink, but it also served as a dancing and recreational venue. Skating, popular in recent decades but now struggling to survive, was then in its first period as a major pastime. In June 1907 the casino was reported moved to a spot near the ocean when James B. Delcher transformed it to a modern theatre. The post card dates c.1912.

Durnell states the Russian Eagle (symbolized by two heads) Restaurant was operated by the former General Theodore Ludijensky who had fled the revolution. He would also open a place with the same name in New York, which restaurant was found in his time at 36 East 57th Street. While this tenant, pictured on a c.1920 post card, was of brief duration, the building had a more elegant past. *Those Innocent Years* reported that prior incarnations included Johnson's Club House, The Casino and the West End Shore Club. (Courtesy of Karen L. Schnitzspahn)

Nathaniel W. Chater, a New York merchant, bought this shorefront house from James M. Brown in 1865. Schenck, the source of the image, claimed the architecture was ornamental, but not elaborate, noting, "The French roof, as here shown, has become very popular, in a great variety of styles." The Mansard's latter 1860s use in Long Branch preceded the style's enormous nationwide popularity during the following decade.

The motel, the hostelry of choice in the post-World War II automotive age, filled the site of the former West End Hotel c.1950. Ocean Avenue's sharp turn at Brighton, depicted on the chapter-opening map, is visible at the left foreground. The site of the West End Cottages opposite the hotel on Brighton, is vacant. Note the ledge on the bluff on which the West End's pavilion stood. (Courtesy Long Branch Public Library)

Robert Rennie, a Scots immigrant, invested a good portion of his fortune made from a Lodi, New Jersey dying and printing works in this grand Second Empire mansion built in 1866 on the lot south of the West End Cottages (architect unknown). After his reverses in the Panic of 1873, the place was bought by Dr. Isaac Lee of Philadelphia, who is identified on the nearby map. Durnell reported that gambling interests occupied the place for a while. Its demise is unspecified. The *Renaissance on the Ocean* is on the site in 2008. The image is from Schenck.

The Atlantic Coast Electric Railroad trolley, first proposed in 1890, was aimed at developing southern Long Branch while connecting the Pleasure Bay steamboat dock with points south. Its complicated history is beyond the ambit of this work, but early aspects include acquisition of a horse-drawn streetcar line and their initial failure to secure a needed franchise. The rail interests succeeded in 1895 after increasing their offer for the right to build. The line, which ran much of its route along Second Avenue, was completed the next year over protests from some seasonal residents who threatened not to return to Long Branch. This c.1910 post card view of the tracks depicts the point south of the West End station where the trolley ran adjacent to the New York and Long Branch Railroad.

The commercial character of Brighton Avenue, as pictured on a c.1920 post card looking east from Second Avenue, is a recognizable forerunner of its character that is still extant in the early 21st century. The greatest change is likely the replacement of the frame buildings with more substantial masonry structures. Note the fish sign of Hennessey's, a long-prominent North Long Branch fishing family. More than a business street, Brighton was a landmark divide of the popular Long Branch of fun and visitors to its north from the rarified mansion district that developed in the city's south.

Ernest A. Limburg either built or remodeled this house at the northwest corner of West End and Westwood Avenues, a property he bought in 1906. The images dates a few years later and comes from the office monograph of builder I.R. Taylor & Company, while Lansing C. Holden was his architect.

West End's earlier station must have been a dismal structure, causing a *Times* reporter to grumble July 26, 1886, "The present sheds are a disgrace to the two great lines that stop here." This Queen Anne style station, which was apparently paid for by John Hoey, was erected in 1889 by G.F. Metz & Sons, Rochester, New York (architect unknown), a firm that was then building stations on the New York-New Haven line. It was located about 200 yards south of the old station. Pictured on a c.1905 post card, this structure was destroyed in a 1921 conflagration that also burned several surrounding buildings. A modest utilitarian structure replaced it in 1922, remaining in use until the station was abandoned following termination of service in 1955. A supermarket on West End Court stands on the site in 2008. (Courtesy of Kathi McGrath)

Firemen's Memorial Park at the northwest corner of Woodgate and Overlook Avenues, when dedicated June 14, 1950, contained a flagpole and dedication plaque on a granite base. Additions were made over the decades. The large alarm bell was contributed by Elberon Engine Company No. 4. Arthur Green, the Long Branch Fire Department historian, indicated that the provenance of the locomotive wheel rim gong is not certain, but it likely came from Oliver Byron Engine Company No. 5. The granite markers for the department's several companies, which are arranged in a semi-circle, were mounted at various dates, most in 1977-8. The Line of Duty Death Memorial Monument, which lists the names of five firemen who died fighting fires, dates from the park's rededication on Memorial Day, 2002. Benches provide the opportunity for thoughtful reflection in a tranquil residential area.

Takanassee Lake, earlier known as Greens Pond or Whale Pond, was made into an ornamental lake through a costly construction project in 1882 that also laid the 60 foot drive on its circumference. In this December 1961 aerial, Cedar Avenue, which runs from the left edge towards the ocean, is still dotted with Hollywood structures. Van Court runs across the bottom of the image. (Dorn's Classic Images)

The Green family once owned most of southern Long Branch. The oldest section of their homestead located south of Cedar Avenue north of the western stem of Greens Pond may have dated from the middle of the 18th century. Schenck, also the source of the photo, describes how in later subdivision, the old place and 101 acres came into the hands of Charles H., the grandson of James Green, a captain in the Revolutionary War who was appointed major general in 1804. Arthur Green, the family historian, knows the house survived into the 20th century, but is not aware of the time or cause of its demise.

Walter S. Green built this house in 1862 according to Schenck (who illustrated it) following the partition of ancestral Green lands, a date affirmed by deed records. The 20-room house, tinted between a sky-blue and a bright slate, was located on the north side of Cedar Avenue on the edge of Hoey, who bought the first piece of the future Hollywood from Walter. Its demise has not been recorded. The Glen Ellen Apartments, at number 273, are on the site in 2008.

John Hoey and Hollywood Park

John Hoey's *Hollywood Park*, one of New Jersey's largest, most elaborate, and in its time, famed estates, is not only gone, but it disappeared with hardly a trace. The names of a street and neighborhood remain and while a vintage tree may survive, but the buildings, including the most prestigious of the city's hotels, and the gardens are dim memories. Hoey attained substantial wealth from the Adams Express Company at a time when express firms were the country's principal carriers of packages. His first of many Long Branch purchases in and near what would be known as the West End was the 48.5 acres obtained from Walter and Mary Green in November 1862 for $9,704. The Hoey tract, nearly all of which was west of the New York and Long Branch Railroad, extended east to Norwood Avenue and eventually totaled hundreds of acres. Cedar Avenue was the main east-west thoroughfare through an estate, which extended southward approaching Park Avenue and north to Brighton Avenue. Hoey's mansion and main gardens, including his huge greenhouses, were north of Cedar. Their construction began immediately after his first purchase. *Hollywood*, named for the tract's many holly bushes, was famed by the 1868 publication of Schenck. Indeed, that book is the source of some of the best imagery, but the place grew and became more elaborate over the next two decades. The expanding gardens included fanciful designs in the manner of Oriental carpets. The grounds, which required an army of keepers, became one of Long Branch's leading attractions. Hoey's personal visitors prompted his building a number of guesthouses. One of the largest was intended for the use of Chester A. Arthur, who succeeded to the presidency after Garfield's death, but he failed to inhabit it. The enormous public Hoey attracted prompted him to erect the Hollywood Hotel and its companion cottages.

Apparent financial irregularities brought down John Hoey. It was claimed he secured loans from Adams under questionable circumstances, charges that prompted his resignation in 1891. At Hoey's death, on November 14, 1892, Adams held mortgages on his property. The firm forced the estate's sale in 1900 and bought the property in its entirety. Adams retained Hollywood Park for some years, but over time sold much of Long Branch's best property for residential development.

The aerial of Elberon and Hollywood, while focused on a major piece of John Hoey's former estate, also depicts a nearly intact row of east side of Ocean Avenue houses. There, Grant's former house is in the center, two to the right of the vacant double lot. Left of it is the James Brown (George Childs/Stella Maris) house, while right of it is Harris Fahnestock's, a McKim, Mead and White design for which no image is known. Charles F. McKim's house for Moses Taylor (see Elberon Memorial Church) is the place with the wide oval right of the white "stripe", which is Park Avenue. The Ocean Beach Club is two to the left of it, while between them was Cornelius K. Garrison's large house. He was the father of William Garrison whose Castlewall should be at the unclear white spot at center right. The New York and Long Branch Railroad is the dark band across the center of the image, while Takanassee Lake is at the left. The picture perhaps dates 1940. (Dorn's Classic Images)

Hoey likely began building not long after purchase. Thus, his Second Empire house appears to be an early example of the style. Long Branch was early known for lush vegetation a short distance inland from the ocean. In the case of Hoey's, "Behind the mansion is an extensive wood of fine, large trees, forming a natural and effective background to the landscape," per the *Times* of August 17, 1871.

Henry S. Terhune designed the early Hollywood Cedar Avenue house, built on the south side of the avenue and a presage of Hoey's plans. Schenck projected its likely future disposal to a gentleman who would find it economical and convenient to purchase a completed cottage. In time there would be about 20 in the immediate area. The cupola afforded a fine view of the ocean and surrounding grounds. The six illustrations given Hollywood in *The Album of Long Branch* may be explained not only by stature as the most lavish Long Branch estate, but Hoey was his major financial backer.

John Hoey remodeled this Green family house after its purchase from interim owner Robert Bowyer, naming it Buttonwood Mansion for its buttonwood trees. Hoey, who had rented the farm from Bowyer, improved its cultivation and converted it into a stock farm for Alderney cattle. Located on the south side of Cedar Avenue opposite Hoey's own place, neither its demise nor the current occupancy of the lot has been determined. (Schenck)

Schenck waxed eloquent over the Hollywood coach house and stable describing two buildings connected by a broad platform, which was arranged for the clearing of carriages and other equipment. The stable floors were laid in ash and walnut two inches thick, while the stalls were lined with zinc and contained iron feed boxes. The upper story was a large billiard room.

A reporter approaching the front of the Hoey house exclaimed in 1873, his remarks in the *Times* of July 26, "…a beautiful view is to be gained. The lawn extends from the front of the house with a gentle slope downward for a distance of 500 yards, with an equal breadth on either side of the pathway."

The Hoey Lodge at 211 Cedar Avenue was believed to serve as a social center on the estate. Built in the 1860s, and pictured on a c.1912 post card, it was one of the longest lasting of the Hollywood estate structures, falling to demolition in the early 1980s. (Courtesy of Glenn Vogel)

Hoey was courageous as an inland pioneer. He recalled, as quoted in the *New York Herald* August 16, 1886, "Everybody said I was crazy to buy this land, back from the water. It was a good while before some of my friends forgave me. I think they do now." This image from a souvenir album c. late 1880s depicts an expansion of the Hoey house, notably around the porches. One writer said of his buildings, "Hotels which look like private mansions and private cottages commodious enough for hotels constitute Hollywood." The reconstructed railroad station helps date the source. (Courtesy Long Branch Public Library)

The flower carpets, a highlight of Hoey's gardens, were described in his time as "a reproduction of Daighistan or Teheran rug patterns in greens and reds." Hoey was reported to have turned one of his greenhouses into a freshwater aquarium, while he was planning to make a saltwater version with another according to the *Times* of June 29, 1890. This and the prior image are from a c. 1880s Hollywood souvenir portfolio.

A construction note from the June 10, 1896 *Register* indicated that the Hollywood stands would be 30 by 232 feet, seat 800 and cost $7,500. Replacing racing with the annual horse show not only raised the stature of equine activity, but helped attract a better class of visitor. The post card view dates c.1912. (Courtesy of John Rhody)

The Hollywood Hotel was simply Long Branch's best, its character shaped by a locale away from the shore. A *Times* reporter made clear on July 31, 1887 that "The few people of the true American aristocracy who now make their summer residing places in hotels are at Hollywood, where they get peace and plenty, freedom from the crowding, loud-mouthed, loud-clothed vulgarity of the beach, and space to sun their souls in something like congenial surroundings." The post card dates from the 1930s.

THE BALL ROOM OF THE HOLLYWOOD HOTEL.

Hoey wanted to establish a winter season in Long Branch, perhaps using Lakewood as a model, but the idea never caught on. The ballroom postcard dates c.1905. (Courtesy of John Rhody)

The office of the Hollywood Hotel.

THE OFFICE OF THE HOLLYWOOD HOTEL.

Hollywood Hotel, West End, N. J.

The Hollywood Hotel was greatly expanded in 1900 by removal of a glass-enclosed ballroom and the erection of a three-story addition in its place, which appears to be the part illustrated in this c.1930s post card. The Hollywood was always at the pinnacle of Long Branch hotels. Ready insight into that standing may be inferred from a chart of room rates from any period – the Hollywood was invariably the costliest. (Courtesy of Gail Gannon)

The Hollywood's 1950 modern entrance is pictured on a chrome post card of that decade. A newly refurbished Hollywood Hotel was destroyed by fire on March 27, 1961. The blaze cost the life of fireman Robert Pearce who suffered a heart attack on arriving at the fire.

The mid-19th century residence at 364 Cedar Avenue, historically the Frederick Behr farm, was in the recent past the home for nearly 50 years of the late Robert and Aileen Connolly. Its entry on the National Register of Historic Places provided an endearing story of individual initiative, as Aileen completed the research for the submission in a successful effort to thwart a road-widening project there. In repeating the account over the years, the author would point out that while National Register listing provided obstacles for "public takings," it was no bar for a private owner doing whatever he wanted with the property, including destruction, but municipal preservation ordinances could provide such protection. The house was demolished in 2008, the year a preservation ordinance was proposed in the city, a law that would be considered "weak" in its level of protection of historic sites and minimal in the potential impediments to owners. Still, as this book is edited in the spring of 2009, support for the proposal wavers among city council members some of whom appear to feel that since Long Branch has lost so much of its historic built environment, the rest is disposable. Others may not wish to inconvenience builders, who, once the present depression ends, will continue building condominiums in the city, a process which made the author wonder if the "reinventing" in the sub-title should have been "destroying." Hope is stimulated by passage of a preservation ordinance by the Long Branch City Council on May 26, 2009.

This handsome c.1880s Shingle Style house which stood at 281 Bath Avenue is obscured not only by the trees in this 1951 photograph, but by its having been lost with hardly a historical trace. Later it was the Westwood Private Nursing Home and the Westwood Hall Hebrew Home. Its destruction date, believed in the recent past, is not specified while the lot at the northwest corner of Westwood Avenue remained vacant at the end of 2008. (Dorn's Classic Images)

The Frank McDermott who bought two Hollywood lots in 1906 was from New York rather than the familiar Monmouth political figure of the same name. He completed this fine Italian Renaissance Revival house the next year (architect unknown) at 650 Woodgate Avenue. It stands little changed on a street that has lost a number of its early houses, although the port-cochere is gone and some porches have been enclosed. McDermott lost his wife not long after completion and remained a widower when he sold the house in 1917. (Courtesy of Glenn Vogel)

A *Times* reporter seeking refuge from his hotel's "hurly-burly" commented August 17, 1871 about his long walk on Cedar Avenue, noting it was "by far the prettiest bit of landscape at the Branch…a scene of pastoral quiet that has many charms." He thought the cedars lining the road were stinted, but having defied the blast of winter. The trees had matured for this post card view taken west of the railroad tracks over three decades later.

The Colony Surf Club was on the ocean north of the Takanassee Life Saving Station. The club and the adjoining casino were bought by a local syndicate, which enabled this place to accommodate casino cabana users after the fire. The main clubhouse was destroyed by fire on October 8, 1948, although some cabanas were saved. Were the dancers on the left posing or doing their own thing? This view of the ocean, as on this c.1940s postcard, now is enjoyed by residents of Imperial House.

After some years of planning, the West End Casino opened its new casino and swimming pools in 1925 which "promises to establish a new social center for the cottages" as was reported by the *Times* on June 25. When known as the Sand & Surf Club, the place was destroyed by fire on August 31, 1965. The last reminder of the casino that may be fixed in memory could be the entertainment hall nearer the street that was host to big-name performers prior to World War II. The prominent pools, pictured on a c.1940s post card, were reincarnated through a later occupant.

When the Sand and Surf Hotel and Cabana Club, built by the Hotel Corporation of Long Branch, opened for the 1950 season, about half of its eventual expected room total of 200 was finished. The builders, which had operated the former West End Casino and Cabana Club, erected the place around its two remaining swimming pools. The hotel was soon purchased by Tisch Hotels, Inc., an early holding of the future huge lodging operator. Larry J. Paskow, who bought it in 1961, promoted the place as a fitness center. Its name was changed to Harbor Island Spa at an unspecified point. (Courtesy of Kathi McGrath)

The late Elene Dwyer told the author the Harbor Island Spa catered to a Jewish clientele and that its pool was a center of game activity, including mah-jongg, canasta, and other card playing. The resort once thrived, as shown in this 1962 image, but fell on hard times by the late 1980s resulting in a mortgage foreclosure around 1987. The vacant place, which attracted the homeless and firebugs, was damaged by a number of incendiary blazes including two in 1992 that caused serious damage. The most infamous happening there was the April 26, 1979 discovery of the bullet-riddled body of mobster Anthony "Little Pussy" Russo. The Harbor Island Spa was demolished in February 1997 to permit construction of a townhouse condominium project. (Dorn's Classic Images)

The luxury condominium Renaissance on the Ocean was begun in 1999 on a 10-acre plot on the southeast corner of Ocean and Brighton Avenues, once home of the historic West End Cottages. Pictured in 2008, the stylistic influence is more Italian Renaissance Revival rather than the "Southwestern style" that the developer called it.

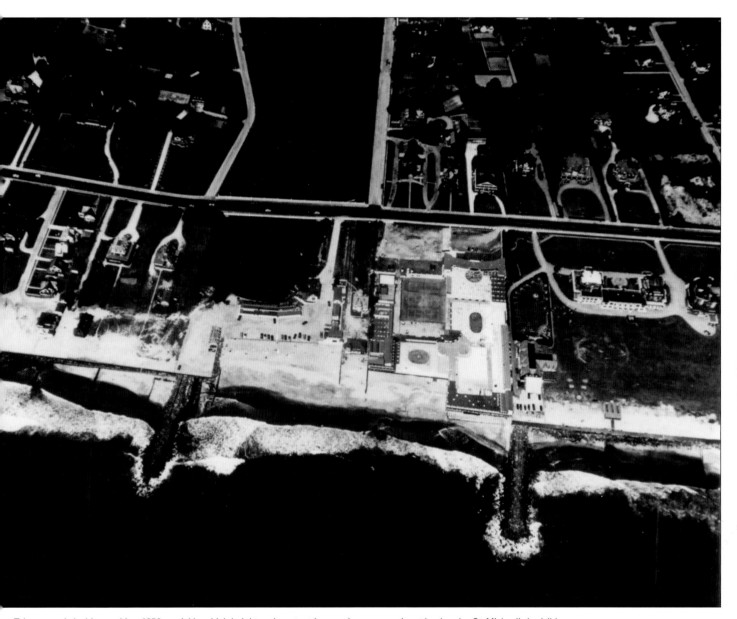

Takanassee Lake bisects this c.1950s aerial in which height and contrast issues obscure prominent landmarks. St. Michael's is visible at the northeast corner of the lake, while the Takanassee Life Saving Station is barely discernable below North Lake Drive. The former Colony Surf Club, right of it, is the site of Imperial House. San Alfonso's, right of it, was still two mansions connected by new construction on the ocean side. The Dorothy Parker birthplace site, on the west side of Ocean Avenue at the right edge, was by then vacant.

San Alfonso – Where God and Sea Meet

The Curtis family, among the earliest summer residents of West End, built three Second Empire houses on the ocean side of the avenue, south of Cedar. The senior member was a lawyer, but they made their fortune from Mrs. Winslow's Soothing Syrup, for which Mrs. Curtis inherited the rights. The three houses have been pictured together, typically after the property was reused for spiritual purposes. The houses belonged, from north to south, to George N., Jeremiah W. and Jeremiah H.; the first and third are sons of Jeremiah W. Their house names reflected the environment, Ocean Crest, Ocean Wave and Ocean Rest.

The New Jersey Redemptorist Fathers had an earlier facility in Atlantic City. Seeking a place closer to New York, they bought two of the houses from Nicholas Brady in 1922, the first of several transactions around their new home. First motivated by Redemptorist founder St. Alphonsus' call for retreats for laymen, the retreat movement was spurred by the then recently (1922) elected Pope Pius XI, who signified the importance of retreats as "the soul of Catholic action." Initially, the West End house was given the same name, St. Joseph's Cottage, as was used in Atlantic City, but to avoid confusion with another nearby Catholic facility, it was renamed in honor of the order's founder. The first retreat was held in September 1925. The center and south house were connected in 1931 by a frame structure that contained a chapel and dining room.

The George N. Curtis house on the north end of the property was one of the two mansions the Redemptorists bought in 1922. This undated photograph reflects the remodeling Curtis undertook on all three houses in 1881. (Courtesy Long Branch Public Library)

Jeremiah W.'s house, located in the center of the three, was the most ornate and probably the first built. One of the two bought in 1922, the house was connected to the southerly mansion two years after the latter's 1929 purchase by the Redemptorists. (Courtesy of Karen L. Schnitzspahn)

The exterior of the chapel, planned to be reminiscent of a ship's bow, makes a striking, instant impression to every passer-by at 755 Ocean Avenue. The 1967 expansion was the work of Connecticut architect Robert Mutreaux who had earlier designed a seminary for the order. The four San Alfonso color images date 2008.

The retreat movement, which expanded in the post-World War II years, overwhelmed the old facility prompting reconstruction in the 1960s. The mansions were demolished in 1966, while the construction that followed precluded retreats the next year. The new San Alfonso Retreat House was blessed by Bishop George W. Ahr on September 22, 1968. Renovation and upgrading followed in the coming decades. In 2008, San Alfonso's, "Where God and Sea Meet", one of the largest retreat centers in America, hosts retreats on 47 weekends.

This marble figure of St. Alphonsus Liguori sitting in a wheelchair, the work of Austrian sculptor Herbert Gunthur, was installed in a prayer garden adjacent to the east elevation on December 6, 1995. He is the patron saint of those suffering from arthritis.

This crucifix near the garden's eastern edge is dedicated to the memory of the Reverend Jim Foley, who served here 1981-5.

Brian Hanlon's *Stella Maris Star of the Sea* sits on a jetty rock holding the baby Jesus who is pointing towards Bethlehem. Symbolism embedded in the work includes the visible fisherman's net, a starfish, and the seal of the Redemptorists. The sculpture was dedicated to Maurice O'Keefe on July 25, 1999.

The first icon of Our Lady of Perpetual Help, dating to 1499 at the Church of St. Matthew in Rome, was moved to a monastery following Napoleon's destruction of the church in 1812, and later given to the Redemptorists by Pope Pius IX with the imperative to "Make Perpetual Help known throughout the world." This mosaic example was made in the Pittsburgh studios of Rohn Design Group in the mid-1980s. It is mounted facing the ocean in a shrine located behind the retreat house. The Greek letters identify the figures of Jesus, Mary and the Archangels Michael and Gabriel, who startle Jesus who is pictured holding the instruments of his passion, the cross, nails, spear and sponge. The startled Jesus is clasping Mary's hand for help, our example for emulation. (With thanks to Redemptorist Fr. John Murray)

Parker was not only the quintessential New York literary figure, but she expressed lifelong complaints about her New Jersey nativity. However, that disdain does not diminish her embrace by New Jersey and particularly Long Branch. The Rothschild house is long-gone, but the 732 Ocean Avenue site is designated as a Literary Landmark by Friends of Libraries USA. From 1953 Parker lived at the Volney Hotel at 23 East 74th Street. She died June 7, 1967, leaving her estate to Martin Luther King Jr. with the wish that it be conveyed to the National Association for the Advancement of Colored People. The estate and Parker's remains make a fascinating story beyond the ambit of this work.

Dorothy Rothschild Parker, born at Long Branch on August 22, 1893, became one of America's celebrated women writers of her generation, specializing in criticism and the short story. An early member of the Algonquin Round Table, Parker was noted for satirical and mordant wit that often touched or crossed the line of caustic. Her career included positions at *Vanity Fair* and *The New Yorker.* Parker's penchant for social justice resulted in an arrest for a 1927 demonstration against the execution of Sacco and Vanzetti.

Parker's two great loves were her dogs and martinis, not necessarily in that order. The world had to take note of her legendary devotion to her canine companions as she insisted on taking them everywhere, unhesitatingly violating "no animal" constraints. Parker's love of dogs is celebrated each summer by a dog walk near her birthplace. The image is Roland.

St. Michael's at its establishment around 1880 as a mission of Star of the Sea served largely a summer following. Completion of this fine Victorian Gothic edifice at 796 Ocean Avenue took some while after the July 1883 signing of the building contract. A basement had a temporary roof in 1884 suggesting early use, while the cornerstone is dated July 25, 1886. Dedication followed in August 1, 1891, while parish status was attained the next year. St. Michael's is standing alone in the merger of the Star of the Sea group described in Chapter 4. Although beginning as a mission of the latter, St. Michael's, perhaps reflecting the elevated demographics of its area, has an enrollment nearly equal to the three merging churches located elsewhere in the city.

St. Michael is pictured on the stained glass over the main altar, which was given in memory of famed Philadelphia banker Francis Anthony Drexel. His daughter Katherine, who became a nun, founded the Sisters of the Blessed Sacrament.

While St. Michael's was named after the Most Reverend Michael J. O'Farrell, the first bishop of the Diocese of Trenton who started the parish, St. Michael the Archangel is their chosen patron. His statue stands before the façade.

An iron bridge built in 1882 when Takanassee Lake was made into an ornamental body replaced what was presumably a frame crossing. The lake was described that year as an inlet of the sea, but fed by a stream and was the source of the Long Branch Water Works. That bridge, in time, was replaced by the county with a concrete bridge in 1912. That bridge was reconstructed in 1950, but the span reached the end of viability by century's end. A new replacement bridge was erected in 2001, this one pictured in 2008, constructed as a replica of the bridge familiar through historic imagery. Its number is O-21.

The 18-story, 221-feet Imperial House, at 787 Ocean Avenue, was Long Branch's highest building when erected in 1972-3 as a high-rise apartment on the site of the Colony Surf Club. That distinction was retained in 2008, the year of the image.

This boathouse from Schenck not only predated the three structures threatened at the book's late 2008 completion, but the Takanassee Life Saving Station was then (1868) identified as No. 4. Schenck claimed the first rescue here was a crew of 18 taken from the *Adonis* in March 1859. It was renumbered "5" after Monmouth Beach was established and given number "4". Apparently this building was replaced, probably in the late 1870s, by a 1 ½-story structure built in the manner of the model shown at the 1876 Centennial Exposition at Philadelphia. The second of the three has a square tower, contained the keeper's living quarters and probably dates from the same period.

U. S. Life Saving Station, West End, Long Branch, N. J.

The latest of the three structures at 805 Ocean Avenue, the Port Huron model, is named for the site of the style's early installation. News accounts point to its date, purpose and locale. The *Times* on May 17, 1903 indicated a new station will supplant the present humble quarters built more than a quarter-century ago, then reported on September 6 that the new station, similar to Monmouth Beach, was begun on the Painter lot adjoining the old station. The reference reflects the station's expansion as this chapter's map identifies Painter as owner of the lot to the north. The site, occupied by the Takanassee Beach Club for decades, has been designated for development, while preservationists in 2008 are engaged in a campaign to save the historic beachfront for public use. (Courtesy of George Moss)

Ocean Avenue, Elberon, N. J.

This c.1905 postcard view of Ocean Avenue looking north from Lincoln offers little that grabs the eye. Comparison with the Ripley painting and the Elberon aerial is possible, but difficult as a consequence of varying perspectives.

The Elberon Hotel, designed by Charles F. McKim, was built in 1876 as an addition to and located on the north of the Charles G. Francklyn house. Located on the east side of Ocean Avenue opposite Lincoln, the new hotel was well-timed for Elberon's greatest period of growth, drew favorable notice from patronage by Grant's successor, Rutherford B. Hayes, and was further thrust in the public eye by proximity to Garfield's place of death. The hotel grounds included about 15 cottages that functioned in conjunction with the main building. Guests slept in the cottages and took their meals in the hotel. The post card image dates c.1910, not long before the place's destruction by fire four years later. (Courtesy of Glenn Vogel)

The Charles F. McKim-designed Charles G. Francklyn cottage, built in 1876, was described by architectural historian Robert Guter as "noteworthy for its sharp planes and linear surface treatments, evidence of stick style antecedents which played no part in the firm's (McKim's later partnership, McKim, Mead and White) work after 1876. It was a forerunner of the Shingle Style, also noteworthy for its asymmetrical arrangement of rooms and verandas around the central hall." The south elevation is seen on a c.1911 post card, with a glimpse of the Elberon Hotel at right.

A second view of the Francklyn Cottage, which shows the west elevation, depicts the charm of a cyanotype photograph printed on post card stock, perhaps c.1910. The inscription merits note, as the house became a veritable and venerable shrine that rented at a premium. For many years it was taken by Augustine Smith of New York. The house, following damage in the 1914 Elberon Hotel fire, was removed some years later.

Catherine A. Taylor built the Elberon Memorial Church to honor her deceased husband, Moses, who died May 25, 1882. The Taylors had a summer home nearby at 1083 Ocean Avenue, which was demolished in 1982. A major financier, among Taylor's numerous interests was control of the Delaware Lackawanna & Western Railroad, when that line was one of the most profitable in America. The church, a fine, shingled, Gothic Revival edifice, was built in 1886 at 70 Park Avenue. Its architect is unknown, frequent misattributions notwithstanding. A Sunday school building is affixed on the southeastern end of the building. Elberon Memorial, while following the Presbyterian tradition, is a summer congregation with an appeal to a broad public, which stems from an outstanding music program. Their pipe organ was built in 1885 by famed organ builder Hilborne L. Roosevelt. More than a church, Elberon Memorial is a community cultural treasure.

Howard Potter built this Stick style cottage at 991 Ocean Avenue in 1867. A prominent banker, his important commission by New York architect Charles W. Clinton is historically noteworthy in its own right absent its later ownership by President Ulysses S. Grant, for whom three wealthy summer residents bought the place in 1870. The house, which was readily visible from the street, became a major tourist attraction during Grant's ownership. Grant actively and eagerly mixed with the public, which created regular possibilities of presidential sightings here. Early photographs, such as this Pach stereograph, depict the original house, although more common are post card views which reflect the remodeling done of 1884 buyers Edward A. and Bertha Price. The Sisters of St. Joseph of Peace bought the house in 1963 in response to reports of its planned use as a nightclub, then demolished it the next year. The chapel on the southern edge of the Stella Maris facility extends into the Grant lot, which otherwise remains vacant. (Courtesy of Karen L. Schnitzspahn)

Architect Edward T. Potter's Stick Style house designed for James M. Brown, built in 1867-8, is one of that period's most important on the New Jersey coast. Brown, a founder of the New York banking firm of Brown Brothers & Co., was only a short-term owner of *Sea Cliff Villa,* at 981 Ocean Avenue, as the place is associated historically with his 1872 buyer, the prominent Philadelphia publisher George W. Childs. A third prominent owner, New York banker Adolph Lewisohn, bought the house in 1895 and likely installed the richly carved paneling, fireplace and stairs still present in the main hall. The Sisters of St. Joseph of Peace bought the place for $14,000 in 1941 and opened a "summer home for Sisters" in 1942 when they renamed it Stella Maris Convent.

Stella Maris, which became a retreat center, expanded over the years. Two 1959 wings are pictured on the right. Two other features that stand out in this c.1970s aerial view post card are the Grant house lot as a clear field and a fine view of a piece of Long Branch's small remaining bluff. A chapel was built south of the main Stella Maris building in 1994. Glimpses of Ocean Avenue and surrounding streets show how little remains of Elberon's early built environment.

Boston architects Peabody and Stearns designed the Elberon Casino, which was built in 1883 at the northeast corner of Lincoln and Elberon Avenues. The casino in the 19th century was a social hall, typically operated as a club for the affluent. This image was pictured in 1886-7 in George William Sheldon's *Artistic Country-Seats* where an accompanying plan denotes a general lounging room located on the left, while an auditorium with a stage, presumably a theatre, was on the right. The building, which retained its integrity in conversion to a residence at an unspecified date, was demolished in 1959 for the later houses on the site.

Louis Long made the Classical Revival modifications designed by Lansing G. Holden to 988 Elberon Avenue shortly after buying the property in 1905 from David and Mary Lyddy. The house, pictured in 1993 and of uncertain origin, remained little changed for around a century until undergoing substantial reconstruction in 2008.

Park Avenue's development was delayed until the mid-1870s because early landowners, including Woolley and West, kept their holdings intact. In addition, Conklin's large parcel was tied-up in litigation with the Market Savings Bank stemming from charges of his financial irregularities. Comparison of the 1873 Beers with this chapter's 1886 map depicts the progress that ensued. The Park Avenue bridge on this c.1907 postcard appears to be the crossing over the New York and Long Branch tracks. Thus, it is the earlier span rather than its 1913 replacement, which is being rebuilt in 2008 in a project taking even longer than this book. The new bridge finally opened in early January, 2009.

P638   Castle Wall, Summer Res. of Myron H. Oppenheim.
West End, N. J.

William R. Garrison, born 1834 in Canada, the son of Commodore C.K. Garrison who would also own an Elberon cottage, went to California with his father in 1853, making money in transportation ventures. Arriving in New York in 1860, the younger Garrison became wealthy from rail and shipping, among varied businesses. He bought a piece of a former West farm from John Hoey around 1880 and commenced to build one of the region's costliest houses on an attractive estate where his landscaping costs were comparable to this enormous cottage. Sited on an elevation north of Park Avenue, between Van Court and Norwood Avenue, a contemporary account described the house as covering a plot about 100 feet square, surrounded by 16-foot piazzas. It had sides and roof of California redwood cedar shingles painted sage green for the former and dark olive for the latter. The steep drop in elevation on the south necessitated construction of the great brick bastion, which gave rise to the name *Castlewall.* Garrison did not live to enjoy his mansion. Completed in June 1882, he died on July 1 from injuries sustained in the June 29 wreck on the New York and Long Branch Railroad bridge over Parkers Creek that connects Little Silver and Oceanport. A number of owners held the place, including Myron H. Oppenheim and the Rev. Charles Hoffman, prior to the property being developed beginning in 1925. The house, in time, fell down.

Lewis B. Brown began his purchase of four tracts from the Woolley family in December 1865 to develop his early venture of Blythe Beach Park, which was located on the south side of Woolley Avenue. He also bought this house, once owned by fisherman James Green, and made an extensive remodeling. The internal chimneys suggest an older place obscured by the 1860s construction of four-sided, two-story piazzas. The image from Schenck's *Album of Long Branch* predates Brown's later fame from his namesake Elberon development on Long Branch's southern shore. The place was demolished in 1901 by Daniel Guggenheim for replacement by a new house.

The Ocean Beach Club, which organized in 1905 as a Jewish alternative to the Christian-membership Elberon Beach Club that had formed some years earlier, owns an infrequent intact reminder of an early Elberon house. The clubhouse, at 1035 Ocean Avenue, was probably built by Amos Cotting around 1880. The Club first owned shore property in 1895. Their complexity of their title history is suggested by ownership of a three-tract parcel on which this building, pictured in 2008, stands.

Maurice Seligman built this Colonial Revival cottage on the east side of Ocean Avenue in 1901. Leon Cubberley was his architect for the project located a few hundred feet south of Park Avenue. Pictured on a c.1920 post card, the house's disposal has not been ascertained.

James W. Wallack, Jr., an English-born actor and cousin of Lester, bought in the name of his wife Ann, a 55 acre farm in 1858 located in the future Elberon. They improved the farm dwelling, an early boarding house in the Green family, on a tract that ran north from Park Avenue to the then-Green Pond. Named Hopefield when pictured in Schenck, it was later called The Sycamores. Following the deaths of James in 1873 and Ann seven years later, the property was developed. A street was parallel with Ocean Avenue was opened, initially Wallack Terrace, later Elberon Avenue.

Residence of Mrs. C. T. Cook, Lincoln Avenue, Elberon, N. J.

Charles T. Cook, the president of Tiffany & Co., built his house on the south side of Lincoln Avenue, one lot west of Ocean Avenue, in 1885. Charles Follen McKim of the McKim, Mead and White firm probably drew the plans. The c.1910 post card view looks west. (Courtesy of Glenn Vogel)

General View — Showing Residence of Mrs. Washington Wilson, Lincoln Avenue, Elberon, N. J.

The New York firm of David and John Jardine designed the Washington Wilson house, built 1886 on the south side of Lincoln Avenue. Its grounds were laid out in mosaic floral work. This house was the last on the west before the railroad. The Beth Miriam synagogue and the Elberon Library would later be built west of the house. Destroyed at an unspecified time, a smaller Colonial Revival house now fills the site. (Courtesy of Glenn Vogel)

March 1908   Business Blocks, Elberon, N. J.

Real estate promoter J. A. Stratton brought commercial activity to Elberon by erecting this row of stores in 1903 on the north side of Lincoln Avenue, east of the railroad station. They were initially intended for summer occupancy. Stratton was not only focused on the area, but at one point agitated for an independent Elberon which he would have linked with surrounding territory then, and still not, part of the City of Long Branch. While there have been some changes in these structures pictured on a c.1910 post card, the block remains recognizable in 2008.

The origins of the Elberon Library were reportedly in a private house, but details are not specified in the 1963 Betty Obermeyer, *A History of the Elberon Library*, its only notable source of information. The library has been located in this modest, but appealing, Colonial Revival building at 168 Lincoln Avenue since 1911. Its architect is not known, the building's attribution to a prominent New York firm notwithstanding. Pictured in 2008, Elberon has been part of the Long Branch library since c.1994.

John Taylor Johnston, president of the Central Railroad, had a penchant for adapting personal names for their stations. Lewis B. Brown, the principal developer of southern Long Branch is the namesake for the Elberon station, from which the neighborhood took its name. After saying "L.B. Brown" often and fast enough, it sounds reasonably like "Elberon." Pictured on a c.1907 post card is Elberon's second station, built in 1899 to replace one destroyed by fire. It, in turn, burned in 1988.

Elberon was initially a stop on the Philadelphia to the shore road, but became part of the New York and Long Branch, now New Jersey Transit's North Jersey Coast Line. The replacement station that was dedicated in June 1996 is pictured in June 2008.

Lincoln Avenue, the shorter of Elberon's two principal east-west streets, bisects this aerial, while Ocean Avenue runs along the bottom. The Church of the Presidents is discernible on the left, adjacent to the fire control tower on the grounds to its south. The site of St. Stephanos is the large lot on the right at the west side of Ocean Avenue. The pictured house served as St. Mary's Armenian Apostolic Church from about the mid-1950s until demolished in 1986 prior to construction of its successor. The Charles T. Cook estate is on Lincoln's southwest corner. Elberon Avenue is the north-south street just above the center. The World War II tower dates the image c.1940s, although its dismantling date is not known. Observers at the tower would radio ship data to coastal defense batteries north on the shore. Ocean Avenue's sharp turn at Lincoln was rebuilt into this graceful curve in 1913.

St. Mary's Armenian Apostolic Church occupied the former George B. Blanchard house at 1184 Ocean Avenue prior to demolishing it to erect this modern edifice designed by Boston-area architect Ramon Hovsepian. The cost was donated by Kevork S. Hovnanian to honor the memory of his mother, Yester. The church, which incorporates traditional Armenian motifs, was consecrated on June 14, 1987 and renamed Saint Stepanos Armenian Apostolic in honor of Hovnanian's father. The church is the center of Armenian culture and thus takes an enhanced significance to the Armenian community, this one serving an extensive area. The image dates 1987.

Saint James Chapel – The Church of the Presidents

The basic historical facts of St. James Chapel are familiar. The edifice was constructed in 1879 at 1260 Ocean Avenue to the Shingle Style design by the noted New York firm Potter and Robertson. The prominent square tower was part of a 15-foot addition to the chancel designed by John B. Snook and Sons of New York, and built in 1893. The house of worship functioned as a summer chapel for the Elberon area. One purpose of its construction was to preclude the necessity of nearby residents to travel to the main Broadway St. James location. However, separate worship facilities reflected the reality of the relationship between downtown and Elberon, which were more akin to hostile foreign powers than neighborhoods of the same city. By the 1920s, diminished support by its wealthy following resulted in the chapel's precarious financial condition. In 1947, the then-vicar, the Reverend Christopher H. Snyder, tried unsuccessfully to have St. James Chapel taken as a national monument. Fading finances and lessened use culminated in St. James Chapel's deconsecration in 1953 and sale for historical use. Edgar Dinkelspiel spearheaded the adaptive use and gave enormously of himself. For years the place was a center of Long Branch historical and artistic activity. However, his failure to build an organization led to the structure's precipitous deterioration. This state caused the author to write in 1998 that the church "is in a deplorable state of decline that threatens the building's survival."

With respect to the Chapel's career as Church of the Presidents, it is claimed that seven: a) worshipped here, b) attended services here, or c) are associated with the Chapel. The author suggests

Most imagery of the St. James Chapel postdate the 1893 construction of the chancel and tower additions. This c.1915 post card view faces Ocean Avenue.

"c." While St. James is an Episcopal church and only one of the seven was an Episcopalian, the Chapel attracted a diverse following, both worshippers and its visiting clergy. The first substantive presidential tie was a memorial tablet mounted in June 1882 to honor the slain James A. Garfield, who died in the Francklyn cottage across the street. With respect to the presidents, the chapel post-dates the administration of Grant, who is known to have attended both the Chapel and St. James, Broadway, and reportedly regularly worshiped at the Centenary Methodist Church during his presidency (*Times* December 7, 1882). Wilson, the last of the seven and son of a prominent Presbyterian minister, has a commemorative plaque at the main St. James to mark his having attended an event there, rather than the chapel. McKinley was rarely in Long Branch during his presidency. His well-known picture with Vice President Hobart at the latter's Norwood Park home was taken during a brief mid-week stop. Harrison's visits were largely after his term in the White House, while Hayes and Arthur, regular hotel visitors to Long Branch, did visit the chapel. More research will be helpful to cement the elusive presidential associations.

In her final years, Edgar's widow Florence, sought outside help to rescue a by-then dilapidated building. The 2001 reorganization of the Long Branch Historical Museum Association brought to the fore activists with strong ties to the city and its surrounding area. They secured and adopted a preservation plan and undertook a phased restoration project that is returning the structure to viability step-by-step. The prospect of the area's greatest historic loss has been transformed into its most ambitious preservation project, ongoing at this book's end of 2008 completion.

The St. James Chapel interior is pictured on an undated Albertype post card. Historical gatherings were seated in the pews for many years after deconsecration. (Courtesy of Glenn Vogel)

The Long Branch Historical Museum sponsored an art show each July. Preparing the grounds is pictured in 1975.

This 2008 photograph shows recent roof repairs and a new painting of the tower. Green was chosen after historical color analysis.

A gas station, pictured in 1958, is so incongruous on an Elberon residential street, but it reflects an era when the petroleum industry installed as many outlets wherever they could. In 2008, the garage remains at 207 Lincoln Avenue, although absent the pumps, located a short distance west of the New York and Long Branch tracks. (Dorn's Classic Images)

The A.J. Riply mural at the east entrance of city hall is hard to photograph, but perhaps a dismal print will motivate some to see the stunning original painting. While a reproduction was in the 1907 Long Branch pictorial souvenir booklet, this view differs. The former focused on West End northward; this image shows much of Elberon, including Lincoln Avenue at the lower left and the Elberon Hotel with some of its cottages at the bottom. Takanassee Lake is the blue band across the middle, while Ocean Avenue runs parallel with the shore. The size of the original permits identification of individual buildings, but even comparing this image with the map at the chapter opening will be useful.

One could write separate volumes on shore erosion and beach access. The inability to control the sea's incursion on the bluff is a dismal, legendary chapter in Long Branch history. The tall wall of sand, suggested by glimpses in Chapter 2, is nearly totally gone. Actually, much of it was deposited by tidal forces at Sandy Hook. The resultant accretions on its north end explain why the lighthouse is no longer on the Hook's tip. Now replenishment programs pour money and sand to maintain beachfronts. This SandMaster rig, pictured in December 2008, is stationed off West End, part of a $9.3 million project, 65% of it in federal funds, that is pumping 700,000 cubic yards of sand. The oceanfront has been too-long regarded as private property in American, a concept and attitude that stupefies most civilized counties. While the American public has long been denied, access to the shore is improving, if one can find the entry points and a place to park.

Chapter 4.
Inland Sections
Downtown and Around the Town

Inland Long Branch was a "small village" in Gordon's 1834 *Gazeteer,* which also depicted the shore as the "much-frequented, sea-bathing place." Differences were also reported by other visitors. In May of 1870, a disappointed correspondent visiting prior to the opening of the summer season complained about needing to resort to village lodgings, which were dismal inns in "the noisiest place in the United States." However, a year later another opined, "The Long Branch of the future will, perhaps, grow-up a mile in rear of that long line of hotels that now constitute the entire place." And so, it happened.

Actually there were two villages and the first cited visitor was likely near the shore, perhaps in the environs of the original railroad station, a street north of lower Broadway. Only two or three blocks separated the thriving shore from a dismal downtown. The optimistic observer was likely around upper Broadway, in the environs of Branchport and Norwood Avenues. Uptown was then a well-settled, active town, much in advance of its eastern counterpart. Other commentators noted that inland lodging near the shore could make for an economical, but uncompromised stay, as the beachfront was only a few minutes walk away.

Inland development was spurred by the New York and Long Branch Railroad, which opened the "central" station in 1875 when "central" was a mere three blocks from the ocean. Lodging and businesses opened in proximity of the station, followed by the hospital, now Monmouth Medical Center, which grew into the region's largest medical facility. This volume's "inland" embraces all parts not falling under the other chapters. Thus, "inland" is not a misnomer, even admitting that parts of Broadway are closer to the shore than westerly Hollywood, which in this volume is part of the shorefront West End. In addition to housing the seat of government, inland developed a business vitality that kept Long Branch in the fore of Monmouth municipalities after its shore's so-called "golden age" tarnished.

Broadway east of city hall, pictured in 1951, shows two landmarks in the foreground, St. James Church at the right and the Garfield-Grant Hotel, the taller structure on the north side, or left. The long, two-story structure on the south side is the Jones Motors building. The split of Broadway near the shore is discernible at a time when the apex of the triangle was built-up. The former stadium is on the shore, right of South Broadway, while a small piece of the pier is seen to its right. This is the area of the Ocean Place hotel and Pier Village. The pitched roofs at the right center mark Third Avenue, showing the post office on the west side in front of the Simpson Methodist Church. Each cited place is pictured in the book. (Dorn's Classic Images)

Broadway runs across the image in this view of downtown pictured looking north, perhaps c. late 1940s, while Liberty Street-Memorial Parkway is the only thoroughfare that runs all the way up and down. The triangle at the right depicts the north-south split of lower Broadway, while a glimpse of Ocean Avenue is visible in the lower corner. Lack of contrast virtually eliminates visibility of the gas tanks at the upper right. The Steinbach Building, later Vogel's, at 199 is the largest building on the north side, left of center, while the Paramount Theatre on the south at 140. when it still had its tower, provide two points of reference on a much-changed streetscape in which much of the eastern stem in 2008 is a redevelopment zone. The lengthy rows of chevrons are newly stripped parking lots, which underscore the reality of automobile travel in the post-World War II mercantile age.

One suspects the extraordinary c. 1915 image was taken with a hand-held camera from atop the gas tank to the north. However, any lack of sharpness is mitigated by the fine view of the lower Broadway area. Ocean Avenue hotels are visible at top left, while the trapezoid-shaped Arcade Hotel fills the apex of the triangle at the foot of Broadway. To its right on the southwest corner of Second Avenue is the former Landmark Hotel, which has a narrow, round tower on the corner. Above it beyond the low rise buildings is the former Congregation Brothers of Israel synagogue. Union Avenue is the curved street in the foreground. The three-story Steinbach Building at 199 Broadway is at the far right. The Van Note Coal Company yard appears to be in the foreground. (Courtesy of Glenn Vogel)

Bifurcated Broadway, north and south, are on the left and right respectively of this 1884 image of the c.1870 Arcade Hotel. Absent contemporary accounts, one imagines the Arcade helped make the area's reputation as a collection of dismal business-oriented hostelries, although such places could offer a vacation bargain for those willing to walk the short distance east to the shore. The Arcade was replaced by a brick business building at an unknown date, but the small Pinsky Park fills the plot now. (Courtesy of Glenn Vogel)

While the workers in the exterior image were obviously posed, this image appears to have been, too. One imagines a more comfortable spot for reading a paper, but who is he? This man is apparently not part of the companion picture photographed on the street. The lot was vacant in 2008. (Both – Courtesy of Robert Schoeffling)

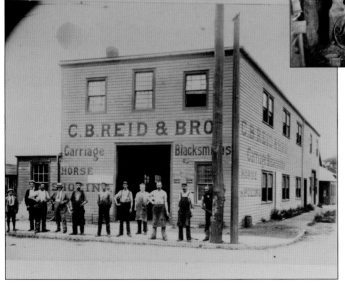

The C.B. Reid & Bro. blacksmith shop at the northwest corner of North Broadway and Long Branch Avenue was pictured by Pach around 1900. Charles and Israel were the owners then. The vernacular frame building, which appears to date from the mid-19th century, appears to have been built in two sections. The Reids were established there in 1877 according to the June, 1904 *Industrial Recorder*.

The desolation of lower Broadway, even prior to its designation as a redevelopment zone, makes the mid-1950s image of a thriving business district startling years later. A.A. Anastasia's Pharmacy was the long-time anchor of the apex of the triangle where Pinsky Park now begins. The dates when these buildings were cleared is not known. (Dorn's Classic Images)

The Landmark Hotel was the final name of the hostelry built by Joseph N. Flannigan, designed by Frank S. Brand which operated under several names in its near century of existence. It was erected in 1896 at the southwest corner of Broadway and Second Avenue on the site of a former Police Headquarters,. Apparently sturdier than the dismal Broadway hotels that the late 19th century press railed against, the Landmark, pictured in 1994, was in faded condition itself, foretelling its demolition later that decade. When examining the lot, which was still vacant in 2008, one gets an impression of just how small the footprint of the Landmark was, especially its 30 foot frontage on Broadway.

The triangular edge of Five Points is viewed looking east. The twisted steel sculpture is *Life* by Michelle Vara of Wilton New York, which was mounted as part of the second annual summer outdoor sculpture exhibition "Sculptoure '08", sponsored by The Shore Institute of Contemporary Arts. A change in traffic flow made earlier in the decade permits access to Ocean Avenue by the southern stem at the right, while the northern stem dead-ends at the triangle's apex.

The former gas holder located on Long Branch Avenue, provides a hint of the locale of Barron & Jarman, which was actually 77-93 South Broadway. The chrome post card dates from the late 1950s. The lot is largely vacant in 2008. (Courtesy of John Rhody)

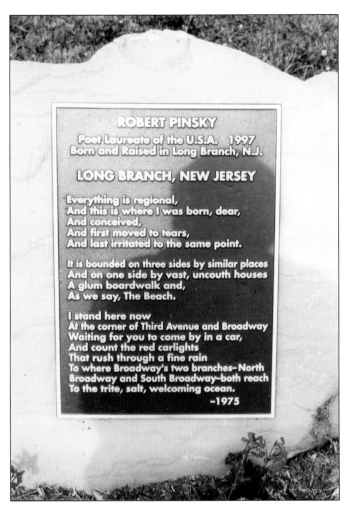

ROBERT PINSKY
Poet Laureate of the U.S.A. 1997
Born and Raised in Long Branch, N.J.

LONG BRANCH, NEW JERSEY

Everything is regional,
And this is where I was born, dear,
And conceived,
And first moved to tears,
And last irritated to the same point.

It is bounded on three sides by similar places
And on one side by vast, uncouth houses
A glum boardwalk and,
As we say, The Beach.

I stand here now
At the corner of Third Avenue and Broadway
Waiting for you to come by in a car,
And count the red carlights
That rush through a fine rain
To where Broadway's two branches—North
Broadway and South Broadway—both reach
To the trite, salt, welcoming ocean.

                                    –1975

BROADWAY BETWEEN LIBERTY AND 2ND AVENUE, LONG BRANCH, N. J.

The background looking east extends to Second Avenue, marked by the round tower of the former Landmark Hotel. The two adjacent buildings remain intact, but later construction to the west is hard to discern in an area that awaits redevelopment in 2008. The Broadway Theatre was demolished in 1930, while the Paramount was built shortly thereafter. (Courtesy of George Moss)

In 1997, city native Robert Pinsky's poem *Long Branch, New Jersey* was mounted on a rock and installed in Pinsky Park. Removed while the park was being redesigned, the plaque, pictured in 1998, was damaged while in storage. Plans for possible replacement with a replica have not been revealed by publication. The park name is apparently informal. Absent a plaque, one wonders about its future.

The Jacob Herbert house was located on the south side of Broadway, east of the original St. James Church, a short distance west of Second Avenue at the bend of Broadway. The place was destroyed around the turn of the 20th century as the area was transforming its character to commercial. Herbert had an active public life and served on the first board after Long Branch's 1868 organization as a commission. (Courtesy of the Long Branch Public Library)

The north side of Broadway looking west towards Liberty Street is pictured c. 1890s. The pyramidal tower depicts the locale of Morris the Undertaker, opposite St. James Church, which is off the image. The frame buildings that then predominated would be replaced in time with masonry. The May 31, 1891 *Times* noted, "Broadway, the main business thoroughfare which leads from the sea to the Monmouth Park race course, is also to be paved from end to end in a substantial manner. The material to be used will be asphaltum."

The Paramount Theatre, pictured in 1946, was built at 140 Broadway on the site of the former Broadway Theatre around 1930 during a time when the area was a thriving retail district. (Courtesy Long Branch Public Library)

The original photograph describes the location of Dr. Henry Hume's house as the south side of Broadway, west of the former location of St. James Church, or east of the present Memorial Parkway. Little is known about the house, but one can presume it was taken down c.1890s or early 1900s to permit construction of the business buildings remaining on the block. The image serves as a reminder of the westward movement of lower Broadway's early, small commercial district. (Courtesy of Long Branch Public Library)

This 1939 linen post card view of Broadway looking west from near Second Avenue depicts the street's two motion picture theaters, including the elegant Paramount at number 140. The structure stands, long-missing its tower, vacant, its former paint occupant having left for this stem of Broadway's redevelopment as Long Branch's planned arts district. The Strand at 135 was demolished in August of 1992; its lot remained vacant in 2008. The image is part of the mural pictured on page 20, near the end of Chapter 1.

The view, a half-block from the companion night scene, looks east from the corner of Liberty on a c.1915 post card, a time when Joseph Goldstein's massive department store filled the lot. On the south side, number 182 at the left remains intact as do some of the buildings obscured in the distance. (Courtesy of John Rhody)

Night colorization dramatizes a prosaic 1940s linen post card of Broadway looking west towards Third Avenue. Vogel's at number 199 occupied the former Steinbach Building. On the south side, Bell is in the distinctive Long Branch Record Building. Newberry's at number 194 reminds of the once-prevalent five and dime variety store, but second story façade changes now mar the building's appearance. The adjacent number 200 retains its integrity, while the Miles building is gone, its footprint a path to a parking area behind.

Most of the north side of Broadway east of Memorial Parkway is a redevelopment zone, but the three-story number 157 is newly remodeled. Notice that in May of 2008, most of the unoccupied street level stores are painted with trompe l'oeil fronts by Bob Mataranglo.

Broadway East of Third

The printed color post card dated 1907 and the monochrome Garraway photographic card from about four years later provide great contrast with the 2008 photograph. The locale is identified by the three-story brick building at number 191, behind the pole in the new picture, one erected between the dates of the two cards. The then-new Steinbach Department Store indicated this was a prosperous part of the city, while the presence of a pawn broker (Loans) is less sanguine, but the business has been there since 1923 and most of the store is now jewelry retail. A Brookdale Community College building was erected on the Steinbach lot, but it is cut-off at the left edge of the recent image. The aforementioned number 191, woefully remodeled at grade, now houses the Long Branch Portuguese Club. Grotesque later facades disguise the two older buildings to its west. Horses and cars co-existed warily in the early 20th century. A 1902 report of a new automobile ordinance indicated a 10-miles-per-hour general speed limit, which was reduced to 5 in the West End. (Color, courtesy of John Rhody; monochrome, courtesy of Glenn Vogel)

The Leon Cubberley-designed Steinbach Building, at 199-203 Broadway, was built in 1905 following their earlier store's loss by fire on January 2 of that year. The appealing limestone and terra-cotta decoration on this brick building is revealed on this 1942 image by the Signal Corps, part of a project to photograph their temporary World War II locations. Then, their General Development Laboratories offices were here. Note the glimpse of the City Bakery at the right. Angled parking has virtually disappeared from the County and street mailboxes are now scarce. (Courtesy, Historian Fort Monmouth)

Alexander Conover's 1927 obituary claimed the family home, which had stood at 219 Broadway, had been one of the last residences in the area to be replaced by a business building. Two years earlier it had been sold to the Citizens National Bank, which erected this fine Classical Revival building. The bank, founded in 1899, had only a brief stay in this office as they were in receivership by 1932. A variety of retail occupants filled the place over the decades. One suspects the building at right was demolished for a street widening because the bank was a corner property by c.1960. The block that was leveled at an unspecified date, perhaps in the 1960s, is filled in 2008 by a fast food restaurant. (Courtesy Historian Fort Monmouth)

The funeral home at 243 Broadway, designed by Leon Cubberley, was built in 1903 for Hyer and Flock. The firm's original name is lettered in the cornice crest, which can be discerned in this 2008 image.

The former tellers' cage suggests a makeshift arrangement for this banking floor's adaptation for a crowded Signal Corp office. (Courtesy Historian Fort Monmouth)

William Van Alen is famed for his design of the landmark 1930 Chrysler Building on New York's 42nd Street. His local landmark, the Renaissance Revival style Garfield-Grant Hotel, completed four years earlier at 275 Broadway, gives no hint as a forerunner. The costly project, the most significant of the city's pre-Depression-era hotels is interestingly located away from the shore and in the commercial district, near city hall. The Garfield-Grant reflects Long Branch's stature as a business center in that time. This mid-1950s chrome post card has become quaint and dated, as it shows in the background this remnant of Broadway's former automobile row, Forshay's Pontiac showroom at number 289. (Courtesy of John Rhody)

Conversion of the Garfield-Grant to office use at an unspecified date left the exterior's integrity intact, although the interior was compromised. A changed surrounding business environment, only partially suggested in this 2008 picture, hardly reflects that a significant hotel would have once been located in this spot.

St. James Protestant Episcopal Church, founded in 1854, built this Victorian Gothic edifice on the south side of Broadway, east of Second Avenue, a site later occupied by the Paramount Theatre. The original board and batten building was the front-gabled section, while the wing on the left was added in 1865 (per Schenck), its construction supported by the contributions of their summer following. The expansion on the right is probably an 1899-1900 addition 78), was built in 1879. The Broadway church relocated to the southeast corner of Slocum Place in 1913, the year after this building was razed for construction of the aforementioned theatre.

The Off Broadway Cocktail Lounge is literally one of the city's most colorful locations thanks to the façade painted by artists known as *The Muralists*. It is true to its name, located a few steps south of Broadway at 12 Fourth Avenue. A half-century ago it was the Happy Hour Inn, which is probably still celebrated, and prior, the Cross Roads Bar, "bar" a short and honest name even in the absence of a crossroads.

St. James moved from lower Broadway in 1913 after completing this Gothic Revival edifice at 300 Broadway at the southeast corner of Slocum Place. Designed by Clarence W. Brazer, the church was published in the May 27, 1914 *American Architect* which described its materials, including Chestnut Hill, Pa. stone and North Carolina pine for the ceiling. The 2008 view of the west elevation conceals a classroom extension built in 1961 and affixed on the east.

Long Branch's automobile row developed on the Broadway blocks east of city hall. The Jones Motor building at number 252 appears to date c.1930, its tile façade reflecting its fine Art Moderne design. The place, utilized by Fort Monmouth for storage in the World War II years, the era of this image, stands little changed. However, it is unrecognizable due to the façade's later stucco cladding; only two surviving tiles over the door hint at its stylistic origins. A flooring firm was the 2008 occupant. (Courtesy Historian Fort Monmouth)

The leafy environs of Broadway looking east from city hall are pictured on a c.1912 Garraway post card. It appears that a glimpse of the Slocum house is above the open gate. The railroad, which would be located just beyond the right edge, denotes the separation of downtown from uptown. (Courtesy of John Rhody)

The long-term survival of painted outdoor advertising signs often depends on their being covered-up, or in the instance of the former Finn Buick at 335 Broadway, the sign later attaining an indoor location. Commonly known as "ghosts", the signs contribute visual variety to the urban streetscape, although a step inside was required to make this 2006 image.

The building known as the Long Branch City Hall for most of its 84 year existence was, when erected in 1891, the Ocean Township municipal hall. The Richardsonian Romanesque building (architect unknown) was described in a news account that year as two stories (apparently an error), 50 by 80 feet, with a tower in its northeast corner. The first floor height was a generous 13 feet, while the second story was a substantial, courtroom proportioned 22 feet. Occupancy included a jail in the rear and a 50 by 60 feet public hall in the second story. Locals were exercised because the $19,000 contract was awarded to an outsider, David Henry of Paterson. The image is a c.1905 post card.

The dignity of the artful city hall at 344 Broadway, pictured in 1975, remained even as the building faced demolition. It was taken down in 1976 following completion of its replacement. At the end, employees' complaints over its ailing physical condition were numerous and louder than the sentiment expressed for the building's preservation. A movement to save it never took hold.

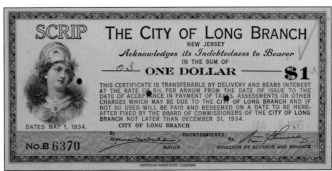

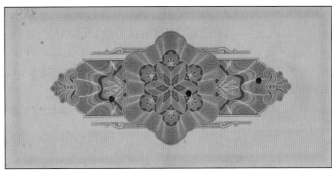

The new city hall was designed by Uniplan, a partnership of engineers, planners and the architectural member, Jules Gregory, formed in 1969 and located in Princeton, New Jersey. While the replacement building appeared fully enclosed when photographed in August 1975, it would not be dedicated until the following July 3rd. Dedication ceremonies included a "wetting down" initiation by the fire department, an event that unexpectedly presaged the numerous leaks and burst pipes that plagued the building in its early years. While employees were pleased to work in a new building, its deficiencies were soon manifest. These brief remarks will not be a litany of its problems, but merely an observation that the building aged quickly, but still endures in 2008.

A public finance crises caused by the Great Depression resulted in some entities issuing script that served in lieu of cash for certain local transactions. Numerous Long Branch examples survive from a time when the city was the County's most populous municipality. While financial irregularities in Long Branch public life could fill a book, one instance made news three years prior to this script. City Finance Commissioner Milton A. Bennett resigned June 9, 1931 and later admitted stealing city funds.

Masonic Hall, at 410 Broadway, pictured in 1991, is occupied in 2008.

Decay threatened Long Branch in the early 20th century. The elements were eroding the shore, the hotels were burning or falling down, while a lack of caring was spreading through the city. The new city government's plan of action was to remake the shore as a family resort, a process depicted under Ocean Park in Chapter 2. A renewed civic concern needed to reach everyone. This undated broadside may be from 1905, if the eight day campaign ran from Saturday to Saturday. (Courtesy of Glenn Vogel)

This meeting of Long Branch sanitation vehicles and personnel appears to date, perhaps around 1950. One wonders if this is the structure referenced in a December 1901 news item announcing the building of a new "crematory" containing a 70 foot stack of 12 feet in diameter. (Dorn's Classic Images)

Peter Pirsch & Sons began specializing in aerial ladder equipment in the pre-motorized apparatus era. This 85 foot tiller (rear-steering) ladder truck was delivered to Oceanic Engine and Truck Co. No. 1 in 1950. Director of Public Safety Rocco Bonaforte is stepping on the running board, while Chief Frank DeLisa is to his left. (Dorn's Classic Images)

Dr. Thomas Green Chattle, perhaps Long Branch's major figure of the 19th century, was a physician born in 1834 at Greens Pond in Warren County. Educated at Pennington Seminary and Dickenson College, Chattle became a physician and professor at Pennington in 1855, when he also relocated to Long Branch. Practicing here his entire life, he took active roles in public affairs, notably education, and served in both houses of the New Jersey legislature. He and the former Emma A. King had 13 children. Also active in the Methodist church, Chattle is memorialized at St. Luke's by this window.

Chattle High School, at the rear of this c.1911 post card, was built in 1899 on Morris Avenue and named in honor of Dr. Chattle in recognition of his strong advocacy for public education. The elementary school in the foreground faced Morris' juncture with Prospect Street. The building in their midst may be the intermediate school believed to have been built c.1909. The Morris Avenue Elementary School was built on the site. (Courtesy of Glenn Vogel)

While public high schools were not common when Chattle opened in 1899, advancing educational expectations deemed it inadequate by the 1920s. A modern school on Westwood Avenue, which was designed by Ernest A. Arend, opened in 1927 and dedicated that October 26th. The handsome edifice, bearing elements of the Collegiate Gothic, must seem like a bargain at $700,000, including ground, equipment and a capacious auditorium seating 897. This building, pictured in 1991, which was replaced in 2007 by the high school on Indiana Avenue, is slated to house the district's alternate school.

Christopher Gregory, who began a 32 year career as the city's superintendent of schools in 1889, oversaw major modernization and expansion of Long Branch's schools. Three years after his 1921 retirement, the newly built elementary school at the southeast corner of Seventh and Joline Avenues was named for him. The fine Colonial Revival building is pictured in December 2006, the last complete year of service before replacement by the new school nearby that retains the Gregory name, but replaces "primary" with "elementary.".

Upon first viewing one of the city's new schools, the author wondered if Monmouth University was returning to its Long Branch roots. The 94,000 square foot, $25 million elementary school unit on Monmouth Avenue, funded by the State of New Jersey, was dedicated in July 2007. Education in Long Branch is subsidized by the state due to the city's status as an "Abbott district." The status and subsidy stems from the 1990 New Jersey Supreme Court decision in the Abbott vs. Burke suit which was intended to enhance expenditures to increase performance in poorly performing systems which were typically located in urban areas. Thus, the state has been incurring debt that is widely viewed as unaffordable in order to pour enormous sums into these districts for facilities that many view as lavish. Their expense is spread throughout a state where rising costs are straining so many local school districts. This glimpse into New Jersey's fiscal crises was photographed in 2008. Abbott funding appears to have been reversed in early 2009.

A reading room on Broadway that opened in 1878 is an antecedent of the Long Branch Public Library. The library appears to have moved to a temporary home at its City Hall environs in 1916 while a new library was planned. Its permanent home was opened in November 1920, designed by Edward L. Tilton and built with the assistance of a $30,000 Carnegie grant, the last awarded in the nation. Library expansion, the first around 1963, more than doubled the space. The fine façade facing Broadway, although no-longer the entrance, is little changed. It is pictured in 2006 following a major preservation project.

Schenck's description of the location of the Edward R. Slocum house on the north side of Broadway at Rockwell Avenue (west side per Beers) is so timely (two years after the 1866 build date) and so clear, that the author will violate a principle and correct a frequent historical mistake by repeating it. This Slocum house was NOT on the library's site. Schenck continued, "The house was planned and built by Alfred Chamberlain of Long Branch", but by the looks, one presumes Al was more carpenter than designer. The house, put-up as an investment, was rented to boarders its first year and was offered for sale in the *Album*. The Slocum family, dating in Long Branch from the 17th century with extensive realty holdings, was developing this place's 40 acre tract. This site is now a parking lot.

This northward c.1910 post card scene on Third approaches Chelsea Avenue, marked by the Star of the Sea Lyceum on the northeast corner. The spire belongs to the former Presbyterian church on the southwest corner, which is obscured by the house to its south. The view is little changed in 2008, other than for later construction in the background.

The Simpson Methodist Church, Long Branch, N.J.

The Simpson Memorial Methodist Episcopal Church, founded in 1881 and named for Bishop Matthew Simpson, was originally located at Third and Lincoln Avenues. They built this Victorian Gothic brick edifice at 206 Garfield Avenue, at the southeast corner of Third (in the foreground), in 1899-1900 (architect unknown). The old church was reportedly moved to Garfield and affixed to the new construction. The vacant former rectory adjacent to the church was proposed late in 2008 as a site for a halfway house. The other dwelling on this c.1910 post card is gone.

The Simpson congregation, which dwindled to 30 members, donated its assets to United Methodist Homes as its remaining members transferred to St. Luke's. The Simpson building survives, although time has not been kind to the handsome edifice which, when pictured in 2008 on the Third Avenue side, was occupied by the Long Branch Church of God. The tower is gone, while vinyl covers the façade's gable.

Painted brick creates a world of difference at 35 Third, especially since the 2-08 image captures the scene before the paint peels. The lengthened first floor windows comprise the only structural change, but the street now has new construction on the south, while a parking lot replaced the house on the north. Although the original occupant is gone, "Telephone Building" over the door still reminds one of the building's origins.

The barely visible painted sign on the south elevation reflects that 35 Third Avenue was built for the New York Telephone Company. The year was around 1912, while the image came from the builder's office monograph.

The design of this fine Georgian Revival post office is credited to Oscar Wenderoth, the supervising architect of the government office. The cornerstone was laid in 1914, while the dedication followed the next May 31st. The Long Branch post office has had several variations of its name, such as inclusion of "city" or "village" and with spelling either as one word or two. Perhaps the most controversial move was locating the office at East Long Branch from 1882-1895, while the downtown office was alternately known as Long Branch Village, then Long Branch City. The building's design reflects the colonial motifs which have long-endured throughout Monmouth County, while the structure's substance portrays the significance to which Long Branch business had risen. The façade is unchanged, while an addition was built on the rear, or west. The 1992 image was around the time of a major preservation project.

This post card image reflects the United Services Organization's World War II occupancy of 150 Third Avenue, the Elks headquarters, located at the southeast corner of Liberty Street in the former Garfield Hotel. The place has been home over the years to a number of other organizations including the Police Athletic League and the Long Branch Recreation Center. (Courtesy of Glenn Vogel)

The small, simple business building at 37 Third Avenue has a handsome façade that reflects 1960s modernism. Pictured in 2008, it was reportedly built c.1963 (architect unknown) and occupied for years as an antique shop.

The c.1912 Garraway post card view (above) of Westwood Avenue (right) at Third suggests an important juncture. The sharp rail curve leaving the station would be off-image, also on the right. The corner building may have been an old store and dwelling, the occupancy denoted on the 1883 map of Garret Robbins' heirs' building lots. The buildings were removed at an unspecified date. (Post card – Courtesy of Glenn Vogel)

The 2008 view (below) shows a bare triangle of land, providing a sharp contrast with the vintage image.

The Long Branch Inn was built at 185 Third Avenue to anticipate business generated by the 1875 arrival of the New York and Long Branch Railroad, a time when its Second Empire style was at the peak of fashion. The August 1979 photograph shows railroad cars that were being moved to the grounds to reflect the theme of the Casey Jones Restaurant. After the restaurant closed in 2007, the structure's future appeared in doubt. The building is not only one of Long Branch's oldest, but symbolic of how the railroad spurred development west of the shore.

The center section of Monmouth Memorial Hospital, pictured on a c.1911 post card, originated as the Central Hotel and was built around 1875 to coincide with the arrival of the New York and Long Branch Railroad. Located on the east side of Third Avenue opposite the station, environs that would be important for the transport of patients, the hospital built extensions on the south (right) in 1899 and the north in 1904. Although the Second Empire style was long out of fashion, their roofs' Mansards match that of the original structure. (Courtesy of Karen L. Schnitzspahn)

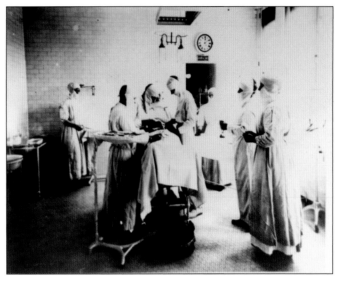

Activity was nil at the former Casey Jones when photographed in June 2008, but a diner opened here in the Spring of 2009. This images looks north on Third Avenue, while the façade faces Morris Avenue. The black and white image looks west on Morris towards Third.

Monmouth Memorial, renamed Monmouth Medical Center in 1958, expanded eastward, in time occupying a full city block. The original structures were removed at an unspecified date. The aerial at the end of the chapter clearly depicts their state in 1962, one that expanded greatly in the latter part of the century. The image of their operating room is undated. (Courtesy of Karen L. Schnitzspahn)

When the New York and Long Branch Railroad arrived on July 4, 1875, its Third Avenue depot, located south of Morris Avenue, was known as the "central station" to reflect its locale west of the shore. Coming with it was an expectation that development would move inland as a consequence of the line. The road, built by the Central Railroad of New Jersey, but for much of its existence operated jointly with the Pennsylvania Railroad, was soon thereafter extended south to Bay Head. New Jersey Transit has operated the line since January 1, 1983. This station, pictured on a c.1910 post card following the loss of an earlier tower, was replaced by a two-story brick station in 1954 and later by the present station in 1973.

Our Lady Star of the Sea Roman Catholic Church

Catholic worship in Long Branch was established by celebration of mass in homes and hotels at least since 1848. The first Star of the Sea Church was built on the north side of Chelsea Avenue, east of the New Jersey Southern tracks, in 1852, but no image of it is known. Their second edifice was the Stick Style church erected in 1875 at the northwest corner of Second and Chelsea Avenues, which was destroyed by fire on December 5, 1926. The church also built a once-flourishing, but no-longer extant, educational establishment. The Star of the Sea Academy opened in 1885 at 152 Chelsea, initially occupying a frame house, but later adding a more substantial structure in 1928. The house had been sold to Daniel Dougherty, a foe of anti-Catholic bias, who turned it over to the Sisters of Charity of St. Elizabeth, a transactional technique at times needed to counter a reluctance to sell to Catholics. The success of the Academy resulted in the opening of the Star of the Sea Lyceum for elementary education. The substantial stone Romanesque Revival building at the northeast corner of Chelsea and Third Avenues, designed by Jeremiah O'Rourke & Sons, included a "lyceum", or second-story auditorium. The Academy closed in the early 1970s; the Lyceum, after the 1985-6 academic year.

The present church was rebuilt on the same site, a substantial stone Gothic Revival designed by Robert J. Reilly of New York. Ground was broken January 28, 1928 and while exterior construction was completed in December, an incomplete interior delayed opening until May 12, 1929; dedication followed on June 9.

The second church is pictured on a c.1910 post card that looks north on Second with its background receding into Long Branch's worst slum, the Limerick district. This was a row of houses owned by Philip Daly, which he rented to Irish immigrant hotel workers. The scant information on Limerick typically comes from later 19th century news accounts of some atrocity committed there.

The Romanesque Revival Star of the Sea Lyceum was built in 1900 on the northeast corner of Chelsea and Third Avenue. While the little-changed school is artistically portrayed in a c.1903 shell-border post card, less-than-clear is its cladding, Stockton stone, a rock-faced, coursed limestone ashlar.

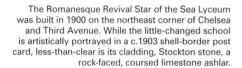

Vincent J. Eck designed this 1928 expansion of the Star of the Sea Academy which was located at 152 Chelsea Avenue. The Academy was early focused on primary education, but instructed the high school grades after the Lyceum opened in 1900. Declining enrollment forced closure in the early 1970s. Reuse as a treatment center preceded a period of vacancy prior to demolition around 2007.

Star of the Sea, in the vanguard of establishing Catholic worship in Monmouth County, is also leading an evolving trend in the consolidation of parishes, a consequence of the emerging precipitous decline in the number of priests. While the number of families in Star of the Sea has declined in recent years, its circle has broadened with linkage to two "national" parishes. "National" is the church's term for ethnic churches that follow the old Catholic tradition of segregating nationalities, but in the modern era, this means drawing members from beyond traditional parish boundaries. Joining the administrative arm of Star of the Sea over the past year has been Holy Trinity, the Italian parish founded in 1906 and St. John the Baptist, the Hispanic church

established in 1978. Three linked churches require only one pastor. This change anticipates the dire shortage of priests which is expected in the Diocese of Trenton in only a few years. As this book nears completion, the Diocese announced in November 2008 that the three churches would merge (rather than link) into a single parish, a process that generally results in a new name. While merged churches simplify administration, the process does not address the shortage of priests. As a historic transformation is underway, one hopes the church will modify its restricted priestly eligibility requirements, single males, a move that would address the real challenge to future needs.

The addition on the rear, or north elevation of the Lyceum, viewed on Third Avenue, was designed by James W. Mancuso and built in 1956-7. The building now houses the Long Branch system's alternate educational program.

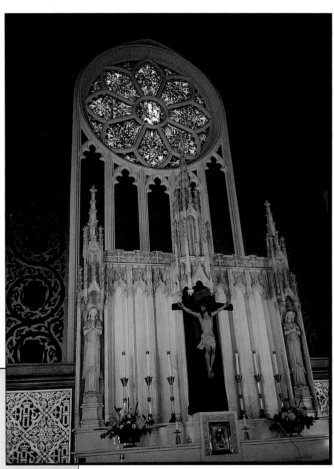

The Star of the Sea altar. A new parish name of Christ the King was announced just prior to this book's going to press.

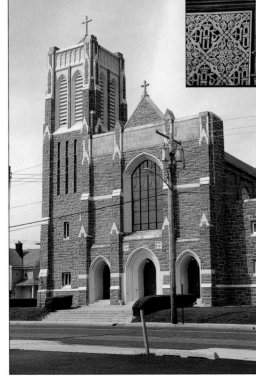

The church is pictured in 1994 following a lengthy preservation project that included repointing the stone. The altar, rectory and convent images are from the same year.

The Colonial Revival Chelsea Avenue rectory, designed by Leon Cubberley, was built by Philip Coyne in 1915-6.

While the Holy Trinity cornerstone was laid in August 1907 and a covered basement opened the next year, the church at 408 Prospect Street, pictured in 2008, was not completed until 1916. (*Register,* June 28, 1916)

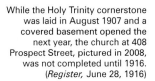

The chapel on Chelsea Avenue was built in 1881 as a private residence, purchased by the church in 1903 for a convent and later converted to a chapel for smaller worship services.

In 1965, a Catholic Spanish spiritual center was established in Eatontown, which in time, was separated into three churches including St. John the Baptist in Long Branch. A former garment factory at 272 Willow Avenue was acquired in 1977, a site that had earlier been McCue's Dairy, remodeled and dedicated as a mission of Immaculate Conception the next year. St. John's, which attained parish status in 1984, is pictured in 2008. St. John's was closed suddenly and unexpectedly in May, 2009.

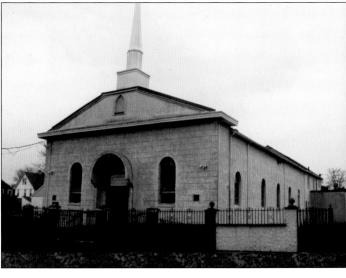
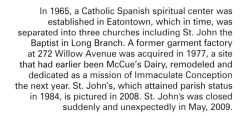

The Victoria Hotel, which stood at 88 Third Avenue, appears to have been the former Woolman Stokes house. Built as a two-story Italianate with a cupola, the Mansard was added, perhaps in the 1870s. Stokes had extensive hotel operations in the city, but neither the conversion of this building nor its demise is confirmed. An undated ad, perhaps c.1920s, claimed the year-round Victoria was "known for its excellent food", noting the grounds were filled with shade trees, a tennis court and tea garden in an appeal to automobile parties. While the ocean was a block away, the distance was short, but the cultural gulf considerable, placing the Victoria inland. The site in now a parking lot.

The two extreme Queen Anne Philip Daly houses, which appear to date c.1890, filled the short block between the northeast corner of Second and Chelsea Avenues and Long Branch Creek, which is now an underground stream. He lived in the one of the left, where his devout Roman Catholic wife Catherine built a chapel, while his son, Philip, Jr., occupied the other, reportedly only briefly. The elder Daly, who operated the Pennsylvania Club (Chapter 2) died in 1910. Evidence of a Manhattan Hotel to confirm the c.1912 post card's slogan has not been found, making one suspect it may be in error. The son's house was damaged by fire in 1942; both were demolished the next year. The site is now a parking lot. (Courtesy of George Moss)

Congregation Bros. of Israel, founded in 1898 largely by mercantile eastern European Jews, initially worshipped in a private home before acquiring a house on Jeffrey Street, one destroyed by fire in 1912. They built this synagogue 1918-20, one rich in patterned brick and stained glass (architect unknown) at 85 Second Avenue and followed Orthodox traditions. They occupied it until a 1977 move to 250 Park Avenue in Elberon. Following the vacant building's demolition around the late 1980s, the site was converted to a parking lot for Star of the Sea Church.

Temple Beth Miriam at 54 North Bath Avenue between Ocean and Second Avenues, founded by the city's wealthy German Jews in 1888 as a summer congregation, remained such until 1939. The temple, named for Miriam Phillips Meyer, the late wife of Sigmund T. Meyer who donated the Bath Avenue plot, was reported to have been the first in America named for a woman. Beth Miriam moved in 1953, aided by a 1948 bequest by temple president Emil Sostman, to 180 Lincoln Avenue in Elberon, where much of the Long Branch Jewish population resides. Pictured from a 1907 city souvenir booklet, the building was demolished at an unspecified date.

A passenger train with two diesels is crossing Chelsea Avenue heading for the station in April 1958. Fifth Avenue at top center terminates at the crossing. The large building on the right is the Joseph Pingitore wholesale liquor warehouse. (Dorn's Classic Images)

Schenck indicated that the Seaside Chapel of the Reformed Church, located mid-block on the north side of Chelsea Avenue, west of Ocean Avenue, was designed by D. J. MacRae of Jersey City and dedicated July 14, 1867. An anonymous buyer acquired the church in 1887 for $6,000 (*Times,* August 21) to give it to the Presbyterians. It was severely damaged by lightning in June 1889, although the reason for the building's demise has not been confirmed.

While Arthur Hearn's Long Branch estate was one of the Monmouth shore's finest, much of its origin and particulars remain buried in obscurity. He began assembling an extensive tract at the southeast corner of Second and South Bath Avenues in 1895, the same year he hired John B. Snook & Sons of New York to alter a house. Precise records of Hearn's several projects, including a guest house modeled after Shakespeare's Stratford-on-Avon home and a massive brick and stone lodge, appear lost. The Tudor Revival pictured on this c.1912 post card appears to post-date Hearn's arrival; one concludes it is the lodge. Later owned by his son James, the estate was taken by the city in 1938 and, for a while, used as a park. World War II housing was built on part of the property, while the last structure was demolished in 1949. Other construction fills the site, its locale still identifiable by a surviving stone fence.

Garfield Court, the first of two public housing projects, was built in 1939-40 around the northeast corner of Rockwell and Central Avenues and was followed by a smaller assemblage for the Grant units. They housed Fort Monmouth workers in the war years, then settled into their intended low-income purpose, followed by a state of decline that ended their useful life by the end of the 20th century. The Grant Court houses were demolished to make way for replacement affordable housing, Presidential Estates, which opened in late 2007. (Dorn's Classic Images)

The Hotel Milbourne, of uncertain origin and pictured on a c.1920 post card, was located at 71 North Bath Avenue, or the north side, just east of Second Avenue. Known by the 1950s as the Casa Hotel, the place was later destroyed, while the site is now part of the Seashore Day Camp and School.

While details of this Woolman Stokes house are absent, the compelling image justifies publication. Stokes' extensive real estate holdings lead one to speculate about a location, but Third Avenue is a good possibility. The tall Mansard over a short third story is grotesque, suggesting that an Italianate house was expanded upward. The foreground figure is unidentified, but Woolman himself is a likely candidate. (Courtesy of Karen L. Schnitzspahn)

The Association Cottage was a summer respite for female employees of New York retailer Siegel-Cooper. The women were sent in groups, 60 at a time, for one week intervals to secure relief from the pre-air conditioning stifling urban environment. The North Bath and Second Avenue location, pictured on a c.1910 post card, was first used in 1899 following a season in three of Philip Daly's Second Avenue cottages (which presumably by then had lost their infamous Limerick identity). The building is the former Seaview Villa, later the Wheeler Hotel, which Siegel-Cooper purchased from Charles Wheeler.

Charles E. Wallack, the second son of actor Lester, was a New York bank president whose career was marred by a major financial irregularity. He built this cottage in 1881 on an ample lot south of Bath Avenue and adjacent on the east to the railroad tracks, a tract that had been a corn field. While described then as "small but elegant", the place should appear of quite ample size to the viewer. It was one of relatively few Long Branch houses to have been published; the image is from the *American Architect and Building News* of February 5, 1881. Wallack survived the June 29, 1882 train wreck that killed William Garrison (Chapter 3), while his house still survives at 374 Sairs Avenue. However, don't look. Blue vinyl siding, the residence's splitting into five apartments, time, neglect and the subdivision of its lot created a sad appearance by 2008.

Lester Wallack, a major New York theatre figure, built this summer cottage in 1866 in the vicinity of today's Second and Laird. Designed and built by G. W. Brown, the distinctive house includes elements of Stick and Carpenter Gothic styles. Schenck, the source of the image of the east façade, reports the site had been occupied by Philip A. Stockton's farm house.

This compelling 1875 picture of a north side of a Broadway store, then three doors west of Norwood Avenue, lacks historical information other than Durnell. He claims John A. Morford's retail business (later under various styles) was founded in 1835 at another Broadway location prior to moving here in 1865. The building was reportedly enlarged in 1875 to this image, while the business remained about another 25 years before closing. The passing of the building is not known, but "three doors west" appears to be embraced by the large bank structure on the corner since the 1930s. (Courtesy Long Branch Public Library)

H. A. Jacobs, Architect, New York City.   RESIDENCE OF MR. CHARLES A. WIMPHEIMER, Long Branch, N. J.   J. R. Taylor & Asbury Park

Charles A. Wimpfheimer, who headed the importing firm founded by his father in 1845, assembled a vast estate on Bath Avenue, locating his house named *Gladville* between Prospect and Westwood. This image of his house, regrettably obscured by trees, was likely taken shortly after his extensive 1909 remodeling designed by Henry Allen Jacobs. The Wimpfeimers were known for their public benefactions, notably Monmouth Memorial Hospital locally. They donated a new wing in memory of their 19 year old son Jacques who died in World War I. Charles died in 1934. The house was later destroyed for development.

St. Luke's United Methodist Church, initially called Centenary, organized in 1861, built a frame church at 535 Broadway, the northeast corner of Washington Street, which opened in 1867. After destruction by fire in 1893, the congregation built on the same site this Richardsonian Romanesque style edifice designed by Poole and Sutton of Newark and built by Randolph and Ashbel Borden of Shrewsbury. The style itself conveys substance, and the size may have prompted Map's diary entry about their having built it at too great a cost. However, they did not built it effectively as St. Luke's was built without trusses or other adequate support which necessitated an engineering solution that resulted in the installation of what might be called a large box framework of I-beams. The little-changed church, pictured on a c.1910 post card, now has a large cross mounted on the tower.

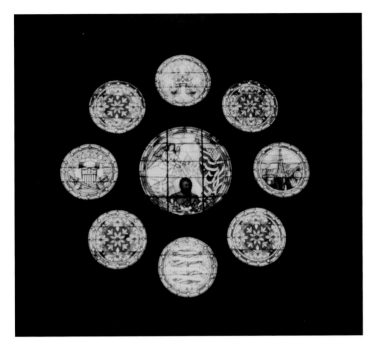

The window honoring Ulysses S. Grant ,donated by George W. Childs, was lost in the fire that destroyed the original St. Luke's. He offered a replacement, but died before its purchase. Contributions by the Childs estate and church trustees paid for this one, the Peace Window, designed and built by Century Glass of Philadelphia. Installed on the east wall and dedicated in 1888, Grant in the center is surrounded by figures representing Peace, Victory and Mourning. The eight smaller windows include symbols of Grant's life and floral decorations.

The west elevation of St. Luke's depicts the location of the former Washington Park at the northwest corner of Broadway and Washington Street. The small park pictured on a c.1912 post card, near the time it opened, was, for practical purposed, a temporary uptown beautification project. Success attained, the park was closed in the mid-1920s when two commercial buildings, which remain on the site in 2008, were built.

The north side of Broadway, east of St. Luke's and now their parking lot, when depicted by Schenck was modern development. The center house from 1867 stands distinguished from its neighbors by its center gable, double windows and single chimneys, each presumably drawing from fireplaces in front and rear rooms, and was built by lawyer J.E. Lanning. The house to the right was designed and erected a year earlier by builder E. J. Pitcher, while the one on the left was built in 1861 by Ann Kingsland, a widow from Deal. The time of their demise is not known.

The Romanesque Revival style Broadway School was built in 1890 by contractor R.W. Hughes on the site of an earlier school. This 2008 photograph taken from the west corner of the façade shows two expansions on the rear. The then-redundant school was remodeled as offices in 1986 to Red Bank architect Joseph Peters' design. Once housing a varied tenancy, the office is now largely occupied by the local board of education. The building remains important to education in Long Branch as a surviving structure from a period of the system's growth.

The poor, pale Polaroid of a short, shabby structure on upper Broadway marks the symbolic end of the author's insurance brokerage career. Being sent in 1992 to evaluate for insurance 576-8 Broadway, which was a dump by any standard and an unprintable expletive in the context of his career, may have suggested it was time to do something else, such as write history. Avoiding the temptation later to toss the image now provided, an object lesson in preservation. The subject building was able to attract two retail tenants, but merely covered its surface ills with plastic, while in 2008 number 574, to the east, reflected a better way to preserve, evident in its fine facade.

Upper Broadway looking east c.1912 shows the Dr. Thomas Green Chattle memorial fountain in the location where it was installed by the Woman's Christian Temperance Union in 1899, ten years after his death. A 6 by 2 foot area around the stone was designated by local ordinance as a "park". The spot is barely visible on this American printed post card, a dismal example showing how the local product, protected by a tariff, contributed to the decline of the early 20th century post card collecting craze. The monument, after having become a hazard to modern traffic (or motorists a hazard to the monument), was relocated in October 1978 to the leafy environs west of city hall. (Courtesy of George Moss)

D.C. Newing owned a large parcel on the south side of Broadway, opposite Branchport Avenue, the probable location of his carriage manufactory and nearby hotel. The individuals are unidentified in an undated image likely c.1890s.

While the soft color of the linen post card (left) has its charms, it is hardly the best available illustration of the handsome 1930s Art Moderne bank at 600 Broadway, the southwest corner of Norwood Avenue. A later two-sided expansion permitted the entry's relocation to the Norwood Avenue side. The 1960 interior may have been photographed to depict a remodeling at a time when bank interiors were being opened for a customer-friendly ambiance. Another financial institution occupied the premises in 2008, but why mention its name as the rapid pace of bank mergers could produce a change prior to publication. (Exterior- Courtesy of John Rhody; Interior – Dorn's Classic Images)

William Russell Maps, perhaps Long Branch's richest man, had extensive real estate holdings including his residential block on the north side of Broadway, west of Branchport Avenue. The first sale was for the corner banking building pictured on the companion post card. While Maps died in 1897, his house remained for some years as evidenced by this c.1918 photograph. He was famed as a diarist. His brief notations of local happenings, made over a near-seven decade period, have been often quoted. The entry for July 16, 1891: "Numbers placed on house doors. No. 517 Broadway" Presumably that number was for this place and was later changed as 585 seems to be his house lot.

Upper Broadway, Long Branch, N. J.

The upper Broadway business district thrived well prior to its downtown counterpart, although the latter admittedly outstripped it before the end of the 19th century. Two appealing buildings are shown on the north side, west from Branchport Avenue, on a c.1907 post card. The Long Branch Banking Company, founded in 1872, built the corner building the next year, one which combines elements of the Greek Revival and the Commercial Italianate. Curious why Maps would permit a bank on his residential lot? He was its president. Adjacent is the 1901 Commercial Italianate building of painter-paper hanger A.F. Golden at number 581. The latter survives, covered in dreadful white paint, and absent its appealing cornice crest. This bank was replaced by the 1920s Classical Revival structure standing on the corner in 2008.

The north side of Broadway in the vicinity of Norwood Avenue is pictured around March 13 following the prior day's famed "Blizzard of '88." That is 1888, as the infamous storm's fame has faded with the passing of the last survivor. Blizzards must meet benchmarks of both snow and wind to be so-classified. While other storms have produced greater snow or faster wind, this ones notoriety and toll stemmed from a populace not forewarned. Many of the crowds engaged in daily activity, unaware of the beginning storm's hazards, were stranded while traveling home, some on trains unable to move in snow. Weather forecasting and broadcasting has gone from a public safety concern to a national obsession. This tuned-out, turned-off author's weather outlook is usually little more than, "What you see is what you get." Of course, he does not go out in snow.

Coast Hardware at number 585 Broadway is among the city's longer-operating businesses at the same location, which appears to be the Maps house lot. The sign is gone, but the place was recognizable in 2008. Much of the streetscape is intact, although the gas pumps were later removed and parking was eliminated for the marking of turning lanes. Note the Chattle monument under the ESSO sign. (Courtesy Long Branch Public Library)

When the First Reformed Church at 646 Broadway was dedicated in 1849, it was a Greek Revival structure with a tower, and a triangular pediment over a classic temple façade. The church was rebuilt in 1901-2 in the Romanesque Revival style. Then, the large cross-gabled wing on the west was added, along with a new tower on the street side. Inspection of the foundation may be necessary to confirm the nature of the work. One contemporary account, the *Times* of April 7, 1902 referred to "new" and "old" churches, terms with varying use in building nomenclature, but the *Long Branch Record* of September 6, 1901 described the project as moving the church backward by 20 feet, to accommodate a 6 by 30 foot addition.

The Neptune Hose Company No. 1, organized in 1877 as successor to Hook and Ladder Company No. 1, occupied borrowed space until this firehouse was erected in 1890 on Branchport Avenue. The construction of the 22 by 48 foot frame structure was motivated by the purchase of this new hose carriage. The building was remodeled as a residence after the present firehouse was built in 1906 and still stands at 20 Branchport Avenue nearby the present firehouse.

The present, larger Neptune firehouse was built in 1906 a few doors to the north at 30 Branchport Avenue. The original building is little-changed, other than for alteration of the entrance following an addition built on the north, one required by larger apparatus. Reflecting the early firehouse as a social center, Neptune Hose fitted their second story as a significant, finely-finished meeting hall, albeit one that, in time, fell out of use. The company undertook a major restoration project that permitted reopening the hall in 2007. It is pictured on March 24, 2008 when the Monmouth County Historical Commission, which aided the project with preservation grants, met there.

Most of Long Branch north of Bath Avenue, the curved street at the bottom of this aerial, is visible, but with little discernible detail. Monmouth Medical Center, prominent in the center, expanded greatly, both prior to this December 1962 image and in the subsequent four decades. It borders Third Avenue, east of the railroad station. On the left, the New York and Long Branch tracks show the sharp curve at Westwood Avenue. The former gas tanks are at the top, while the tower below and to the right of it depicts the Star of the Sea Church at the northwest corner of Chelsea and Second Avenues. The oval to its right outlines the former track, but Long Branch Stadium is gone. The "x" at the right is formed by the juncture of the former New Jersey Southern Railroad (later Central) with Second Avenue. (Dorn's Classic Images)

Chapter 5
Greater Long Branch
History Beyond Present Borders

While now viewed within its municipal borders, Long Branch had a historical reach which embraced an area now in five neighboring municipalities. This chapter depicts sites located in Ocean Township and the boroughs of Deal, Monmouth Beach, Oceanport, and West Long Branch. The buildings are outside the city, but were once within the economic and social orbit of historical Long Branch. Included are two former mansions now part of Monmouth University, the National Historic Landmark Shadow Lawn, and Murry Guggenheim's place. The latter was built as part of Norwood Park, Norman Munro's exclusive development, which was the setting for spacious houses with a planned, vibrant community life.

Norwood Park

The name Norwood survives as a road, which, in part, is a border that separates Long Branch from two of its neighbors. The residential survivors of Norwood Park dot its landscape, but the social and recreational reminders of this summer country colony are gone. Proximate by both physical and lifestyle standards to Hollywood, the two did not fulfill the projections around the turn of the 20th century that they might merge. Now the one-time enclaves are separated by the West Long Branch municipal border.

South Elberon

Elberon's cachet inspired South Elberon, which became part of the Borough of Deal when the latter was formed from Ocean Township in 1898.

Oakhurst and Manahassett Park

The Ocean Township segment of historical Long Branch included much of the latter's entertainers' colony in Oakhurst. Imprecise early geographical reference confused Monmouth Beach with Long Branch, but one development, Manahassett Park, spanned the two. In addition, prominent resident-investor and noted actor, Oliver Doud Byron, erected his dozen houses on both sides of the city-borough border.

Galilee

The fishermen who resided in North Long Branch and fished out of the nearby Galilee section of the future Monmouth Beach were hardly aware of the local border.

Monmouth Parks, One & Two

The original Monmouth Park was the effectively the Long Branch racetrack, although erected outside its borders. While the present Monmouth Park in Oceanport was not given a Long Branch connotation, its grounds are located in the former Elkwood Park, once a sporting field that was clearly in the Long Branch orbit. In short, this chapter embraces places called "Long Branch" in historical references, but which are now known by their contemporary municipal locales.

A cloud of dust is visible during *The Race at Monmouth Park*, from a stereo view by published by the Littleton (NH) View Company (Courtesy of Karen L. Schnitzspahn)

The main gate to the original Monmouth Park was regularly photographed. This image was engraved from an A.J. Russel image and published July 13, 1872 in *Frank Leslie's Illustrated Newspaper*.

The original Monmouth Park, or One, was built in rural environs outside the boundaries of Long Branch, but both its existence and location stemmed from its being within the economic, political and social orbit of the city. Patronized by both the Long Branch hotel crowd and day-trippers, an analysis of early patronage would be illuminating, especially since once the track and its following were gone, they were hardly missed in Long Branch. Monmouth Park Two, also located outside the city, was erected at another Long Branch outpost, Elkwood Park. Monmouth Park One, which opened July 30, 1871, was an immediate success. Its huge stands held throngs that included everyone from the high-tone set to pickpockets. The crowds could overwhelm the hotels and overload the vessels necessary for the transport of daily visitors. While the first season was a mere five days, Monmouth Park was soon established as one of America's premier racing venues. The season opening, typically July 4, drew coverage by the New York press. Building on success, a new track was laid-out in 1890 on the old grounds as the park entered its third and, unexpectedly, its last decade. The state was embattled in anti-gambling fervor in the early 1890s. Local opposition was led by Asbury Park "purist" James A. Bradley, but greater animosity was directed northward to the Hudson County crowd that dominated the nefarious Guttenburg track. After betting was outlawed in 1893, Monmouth Park closed at that season's end. There are historical accounts that claim the track's closure was a factor in Long Branch's decline, but

they are superficial and wrong, a matter explained in Chapter 2.

The second Monmouth Park may make promotional and historic links to the original, but it is a singular and distinct operation. The two are separated by a half-century of time, but spanned by the one-time statewide antipathy to pari-mutuel wagering. Monmouth Park Two had to turn-around the political environment that killed Monmouth Park One in order to be established. The foremost local advocate for the resumption of racing was Amory L. Haskell of Middletown, a leading figure in recreational-sporting equestrian circles. Frank Hague, longtime mayor of Jersey City and a major power in Democratic political circles, was a driving force in the public arena. At times, he virtually ruled the state in an era when his stand-ins frequently held the governorship. The key public motivation to legalize betting was tax income, potentially significant at a time when New Jersey was one of the poorest-financed state governments in the nation. While the approval process for the new park was secured around 1940, the intervention of World War II delayed construction. The new track was located at Highway 36, Port-au-Peck and Oceanport Avenues in that borough, and opened in 1946, although the clubhouse was not completed until the following year. A family-friendly environment and aesthetics have elevated Monmouth Park to high repute. Each August the Park runs a major stakes race, the Haskell Invitational, named for its leading founding father.

The grounds of the original Monmouth Park became Fort Monmouth beginning in 1916. A small workout track is readily visible in this undated photograph. (Courtesy Electronics Museum, Fort Monmouth)

Monmouth Park was given an extensive and costly refurbishment in 2007 preparatory to its hosting the prestigious Breeders Cup races. Still, as this book is completed in 2008, the Park faces major competition from other forms of gambling, some of which run at other tracks. In addition, the thoroughbred industry, important to Monmouth County's economy, faces challenges on environmental issues and on the ethical treatment of horses. The author's memory is forever seared by a death on the track on his first-ever visit in 2003.

A wide-angle view taken in 1985 presents an unusual perspective of the second Monmouth Park.

The Elkwood Park Association sponsored various athletic events on Philip Daly's Elkwood Park, a 100-plus acre tract that he bought in 1895. They planned to replace the wagering-oriented Monmouth Park with an environment friendly to genuine sport, at a time when Daly still had his shore gaming house. Their horse racing and trap shooting activities helped the park attract a better element, but it never found a long-term following. Walter and Frederick Lewisohn bought the place from Daly in 1905 for use as a country estate. This clubhouse was apparently a collaborative design of Joseph Swannell and Clarence W. Smith, whose names are on the building contract, and Henry S. Terhune who affixed his label on the specifications. It was described when new in an 1896 press account when new as 40 by 70 feet with two wings, each 21 by 30 feet.

Elkwood Park's history is forever sullied, soiled and disgraced by its short, miserable ownership by forces of or associated with the Ku Klux Klan. It was the site of their 1924 convention, alternately called a Klonklave or a Klonero, and later for a spell their local headquarters. Walter Lewisohn, at the time a lunatic, and his guardian sold the property to J. William Jones and Oliver G. Frake in 1924. By July, the KKK planned for 80,000 visitors, but fewer than a quarter of that number attended. When they paraded through downtown Long Branch on the fourth, the streets, windows and roofs were lined with onlookers curious about the KKK brand of hatred. This was the "new Klan", which in the north targeted Jews and Catholics to an even greater extent than African Americans.

The long rows of cars from Pennsylvania, Delaware, as well as New Jersey, that lined the grounds provided sleeping space for some as well as transport. Park buildings had limited capacity, so tents were raised all about. Guards, who were stationed at entrances, met would-be visitors with hostility. Local Klan tactics included en-masse visits to churches in which generous collection plates were the intended offset to their grotesque, hooded, fear-inspiring appearance. Al Smith, the Catholic governor of "Jew York", as the Klan called it, and his presidential ambitions were particular targets of Klan animosity that year. It has been claimed that this rally was the origin of Jewish disenchantment with Long Branch. The crowds began leaving on the fifth. Their meeting continued here, but the focus of Monmouth Klan activity soon moved to Wall Township. Both images are from the July 4, 1924 rally.

Shadow Lawn, One & Two

The history of Shadow Lawn is at times conflated due to the Woodrow Wilson association. Their ownership connection, Hubert and Maysie Parson, is one of Long Branch's strangest couples. The Wilson tie resulted from the president having made Shadow Lawn One his 1916 summer White House, while its replacement is named Woodrow Wilson Hall. John A. McCall, who had been spending summers nearby at Norwood Park, bought four parcels in 1902 located around the Norwood and Cedar Avenue area as he planned construction of a new country house. Two were from the Hulicks, a third from the Henderson widow and a fourth from Maggie Mitchell (then Margaret Paddock Abbott Mace). McCall, born 1849 in Albany, New York, rose from a bookkeeper at Connecticut Mutual Life Insurance Company and a spell as examiner in the office of the New York Superintendent of Insurance, to the presidency of New York Life Insurance Company. He earned esteem as one of the industry's leading figures. Architect Henry G. Creiger designed a huge mansion and related estate buildings, the former dominated by its over-sized Neo-Classical portico. However, strip way the extensive porches and cupolas, there appears the rectangular plan of an Italian Renaissance Revival house. The estate soon attained repute as one of the region's greatest showplaces. McCall had a short stay stemming from his loss of employment as a consequence of a life insurance scandal that impacted three leading companies, seemingly over practices that appeared rife throughout the industry.

While beyond the ambit of this work, it appears that remedying those abuses led to New York's leadership in insurance regulation. After brief 1906 ownership by Myron Oppenheim (who had been around to "rescue" Castle Wall of Chapter 3), Shadow Lawn passed that year to Abraham White (nee Swarts). Often known by the ridiculing sobriquet "Postage Stamp" White for having secured major bond issues with no backing, their having been won solely on the paper of his mailed bid, he made and lost several fortunes. White was here only long enough to change the estate's name to White Park as his place was foreclosed in 1908 when Oppenheim again rose to the fore. In 1909, Joseph B. Greenhut, who made a fortune in retail, became the second owner to establish a prominent, personal historic identity.

William Henderson was a member of the Long Branch theatrical community through theatre management and ownership. He had been active in a number of cities prior to working several years in Pittsburgh before coming to the New York area in the 1860s. Henderson bought c.1865 a 50 acre farm from Russell Hulick on the south side of Cedar Avenue, which he called Rosedale. He added land, while expanding the house. Pach found a group present when photographing Rosedale for Schenck's *Album.* Henderson's family included wife Esther, a noted actress and at least one son, Frank. In his later years, Henderson had acquired ownership of the Academy of Music in Jersey City; he died in 1889. His widow sold the Cedar Avenue property to John A. McCall in 1902 for his Shadow Lawn.

Main Stairway, Shadow Lawn, Summer Capitol. Long Branch, N. J.   92-4

The large court of a reported 70 by 89 feet, which dominated the center of the house, was topped 60 feet above with a glass dome. This 25-feet-wide staircase, pictured on a c.1910 post card, led to a mezzanine lounging room. The palatial reputation of Shadow Lawn One likely stemmed more from its interior. The extant hall of Two was inspired by this predecessor. The house was published in the October 1904 *Architectural Record.*

SHADOW LAWN, THE NEW SUMMER WHITE HOUSE, LONG BRANCH, N. J.

Shadow Lawn was soon esteemed one of the region's great palatial showplaces. However, merely extensive porches and bulky cupolas appear to provide the exterior "ornate" image. The post card slogan helps provide a 1916 date when throngs gathered here on September 2, for President Wilson's acceptance of his party's nomination for a second term. The event was called Notification Day when custom had that speech given some time after the nominating convention. Incidently, the term "summer White House" appears to have first been used in the early 1890s for President Harrison's place in Cape May.

Any disproportionate recognition of the White Park name stems from its short tenure coming at the height of the post card craze. The quaint garage on this c.1907 example is not nearly as odd as Abraham White's practice of winning major securities issues with no financial backing.

The Quaint Auto Garage, White Park. Long Branch, N. J.

The south elevation of Shadow Lawn is the more frequently photographed as it faces an open lawn. The north elevation is at least as interesting, but the crowded environment makes it more difficult to capture a good image. This photograph is dated 2008.

The Aztec Solarium was one of the greater of the pits in which Maysie funneled money for useless change orders during construction. The room pictured in a June 1940 image by W. Edmund Kemble was recognizable after conversion to school office use. (Kemble)

He restored the Shadow Lawn name and might also have been a short-term owner. Local interests, ruing a drop in Long Branch's prominence stemming from the loss of presidential association, hatched plans to offer Shadow Lawn to President William Howard Taft for a summer retreat, and to acquire the place for the government as a permanent summer White House. The Tafts, who had a place in Beverly Massachusetts, were uninterested. When prominent Long Branchers tried again with Wilson, they offered Shadow Lawn without cost to him or the government, but the president's acceptance for 1916 was predicated on paying a fair rental. While the United States had not yet been drawn into the Great War, the world was in crises and as a consequence, Wilson stayed home for his re-election. Wilson's conducting his 1916 campaign from the porch of Greenhut's mansion is a well-known chapter of his presidential history.

Hubert Templeton Parson rose through the ranks of the once-giant retailer to become Frank W. Woolworth's designated successor. He bought Shadow Lawn in 1918 and built the present building after the original was destroyed by fire on January 7, 1927. The story of its excesses is also familiar, as is the eccentric couple that oversaw what would be dubbed as the "Versailles of America." Hubert and Maysie, who aspired to social recognition through a grand house, hired country house specialist Horace Trumbauer; in recent years, credit for this project has been shared with his chief of design, Julian Abele, who is regarded as American's first African

American professional architect. Trumbauer was distinguished for his country house commissions along Philadelphia's Main Line; the Elms in Newport, Rhode Island; Duke University; and, locally, St. Catharine Roman Catholic Church in Spring Lake. The Parson project was plagued by owner interference and design changes during construction; some of them were whimsical or ill-conceived. The Parsons, who spent lavishly on furnishings, ran the total cost to about $10,000,000, which for decades stood as the costliest house in Monmouth County. Their lack of social standing was pitifully demonstrated by the locals, who shunned their 1930 opening reception. Hubert's pride of ownership was marred by his swift decline, prompt after his loss of a $650,000 salary resulting from mandatory retirement from Woolworth at age 60, and the great Depression's decimation of his investments. They left in 1938 when Shadow Lawn was foreclosed, but managed to retain furnishings for a notable June 1940 auction. Parson died of a heart attack two weeks later. Following a number of brief incarnations, Shadow Lawn is now Woodrow Wilson Hall of Monmouth University and was designated a National Historic Landmark in 1985. Its naming for the president, although it is not the building he occupied, tends to conflate the history of the two Shadow Lawns. The place received popular cognizance in the public eye as the set for Daddy Warbucks' mansion in the 1982 film *Annie*.

This miscellaneous art object was one of many images made by W. Edmund Kemble in early Kodachrome, taken in the week prior to the auction of the Parsons' contents. He organized a slide show and for many years Ed delighted in telling the story of how he made a pest of himself setting up lights and tripod in the midst of sales personnel who were preparing the place for the auction. The film was slow, but the rich colors held up for decades. He would make others an occasional copy, almost begrudgingly, but one suspected he wanted his work remembered. Ed lent the collection while suffering a decline in his later years, did not get it returned, so the status of this treasure trove of the decorative arts is probably lost or stolen. (Courtesy of W. Edmund Kemble)

Francis S. Chanfrau, born 1824 and known as Frank, attained stage prominence with the role of Mose, a Bowery boy. He acquired this farm house on the north side of Cedar Avenue at Elmwood around the 1860s which he named *The Nest*. Frank was married to actress Henrietta Baker who performed under the stage name of Mrs. Frank Chanfrau. Following his death in 1884, she sold the property four years later to Norman Munro who was developing Norwood Park. The house was destroyed by fire in 1965.

Norwood Park

Norman L. Munro, a wealthy, successful publisher, planned an exclusive summer residential colony inspired by Hoey's Hollywood, which it abutted. He began with the 1885 purchase of the Mary Anderson property with about nine acres and added a number of tracts, which totaled about 250 acres. The appealingly landscaped grounds, included a saddle track and several sporting fields. Munro built a fine home, naming it *Normahurst* for his daughter Norma L. One could enjoy commanding views of the surrounding area from a 150-foot tall observation tower, which apparently was the highest inland structure then in the county. Social life was centered at a hall known as the casino. Munro built numerous houses that he rented either furnished or not, while he also provided lots for buyers who opted to build on their own. Twenty cottages were erected for the 1889 opening. In a self-congratulatory 1891 brief history, Norwood Park claimed to offer occupants, "all the conveniences to which they are accustomed in their city home." Were safety a concern (perhaps from the Monmouth Park riff-raff), "The Park is guarded both day and night by efficient watchmen."

Munro's reign was cut short by death in 1894. His widow Henrietta retained *Normahurst* for rental, including the 1899 season to Vice President Garrett Hobart, but lost the house in a mysterious fire on March 17, 1902. She settled on a farm in southwestern Middletown Township the next year. Control of the Norwood Park Association left the family and, in time, the property was parceled out to individual homeowners. The Association was dissolved in 1928.

Norwood Park, while within the economic and social sphere of Long Branch, was located within Eatontown when established, but became part of the Borough of West Long Branch when the latter was incorporated in 1908. The idea of linking Norwood Park with Hollywood Park was advanced, but it never materialized. Some of Munro's original cottages survive in an area north of Cedar and west of Norwood Avenues.

Murry Guggenheim of the famed copper mining family, after buying the site of *Normahurst* on the northwest corner of Cedar and Norwood Avenues in 1903, hired Carrere and Hastings to build this Beaux-Arts mansion, one completed in 1905. Thomas Hastings, the design partner, became steeped in the shore from his clergyman father, also Thomas, who shared a summer estate in Rumson with equally-famed fabric magnate M.C.D. Borden for whom the architect designed a striking, still-standing carriage house-stable. He also designed in that town the landmark Presbyterian church and a riverfront house, as well as the horse farm seat of William Payne Thompson in nearby Lincroft, Middletown Township. The great firm's best-known commission is likely the New York Public Library, but their Medal of Honor of the New York Chapter of the American Institute of Architects was awarded in 1906 for the Guggenheim residence. The Murry and Leonie Guggenheim Foundation donated the house to Monmouth College in 1960 following her death the prior year. It has served the now-university as their namesake library since 1961. The post card is c.1906.

Norman L. Munro, born 1842 in Nova Scotia, moved to New York to publish. Beginning in 1873 he enjoyed success with a number of publications that reached a popular readership, but his passion was racing fast motor yachts, including the best, the *Norwood.* Munro's premature death in 1894 followed an operation for appendicitis. He left a widow, Henrietta, and two children, Norma and Henry. Munro, a major contributor to St Luke's, is memorialized there by this stained glass window.

Julian Mitchell, born in 1854, rose in the theatre from a beginning as call boy, to staging his first musical at age 20 (in which he also danced) to become one of its great directors. Among his credits were 13 of 19 Ziegfeld Follies productions and 11 of Victor Herbert's operettas. He married the famed acrobatic dancer Bessie Clayton in 1907 as they were building this summer house at 344 Norwood Avenue. Their distinguished architect was Charles A. Rich and not the famed figure to whom the place has long-been attributed. In the crazed world of architectural historical blundering where anyone feels free to say anything, too often the onus of proof is on the corrector. In this instance, documentary evidence is readily accessible in the Monmouth County Archives. See the several Mitchell building contracts filed in 1906. Bessie and Julian divorced in 1924; he died in 1926. The house, pictured in 1991, looked little-changed at publication, although in need of painting.

Several of the approximate dozen of the Norwood Park cottages that survive are situated on Hollywood Avenue. This example, 376 Norwood Avenue, at the northwest corner of Hollywood, is typical of the large, box-like structures that characterize the group. They fall short of an artistic standard that one would have expected in view of Munro's aspirations. Most were designed by architect-builder James Britton while he was working for James Cloughly & Son. Evidently more carpenter than designer, Britton worked at the end of the era when a carpenter who could draw might fashion himself an architect.

Dan Rice – The Most Famous Man You've Never Heard Of

Actually, more have heard since the 2001 publication of David Carlyon's exhaustively researched biography of the same title. That work underscores how fame is fleeting, but provides a major assist in restoring to public cognizance America's most renowned 19th century clown. However, calling Rice merely a clown is the equivalent of a sports biographer labeling Jim Thorpe a great outfielder. Rice was born 1823 in New York to parents perhaps not united by matrimony, a union broken up by his maternal grandfather. His mother, Elizabeth Rice raised him in what became West Long Branch. He left for Pittsburgh in the 1840's to commence a showman's career engaging in song, pig tricks, and strongman acts. Rice, whose success soared in the 1850's, was famous by the next decade, the apex of his career. He was a talking clown, but his clown may be incomprehensible to us now because the contemporary silent, "evil" clown is so fixed in our consciousness. He discussed the subjects that were on the populace's minds, and engaged them with incisive social and political commentary. The deportment of the circus of that era may also be incomprehensible within our current context. Its rough, violent and sexy content was unavailable in polite circles; it was raunchy adult entertainment. At that time, the contemporary circus performance was known as an equestrian exhibition; the word circus itself was typically a type of building. Carlyon

points out that Rice, although pugnacious with a history of fisticuffs and litigation, was "otherwise likable." How nice! Although this background was hardly a resume-builder for a political career, in 1864, while arguably at the peak of his reknown, Rice, a Democrat, ran unsuccessfully for the Pennsylvania Senate. He was a strong opponent of Lincoln, which suggests that any ostensible ties to the President are spurious. Financing for Rice's circus waned around then, which led to a steady decline of his career. While he worked at times in the 1870's, alcoholism became a challenge. He lectured into the next decade, but life became a struggle. Virtually homeless in New York in the 1890s, he returned to West Long Branch, where he was given a home by Maria Brown. Rice died there in February 1900.

Why did Rice's reputation evaporate? One key factor is the changing cultural landscape where "circus" became low-brow. This diminished the greater role of circus in popular entertainment and made it easier to forget.

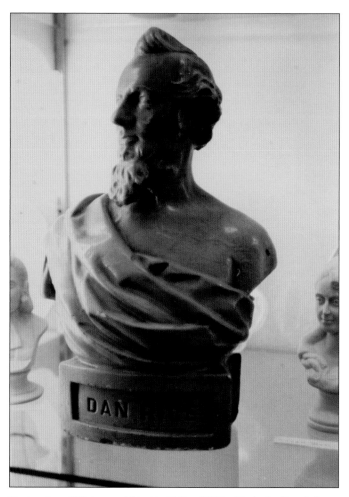

The location of this bust, exhibited in 1976 at Old First Methodist Church, is now unclear. Carlyon believes it is the bust sculpted by Leonard W. Volk and exhibited with a companion piece of Lincoln at a Civil War sanitary fair.

A second may be his life's story which degraded into myth. In addition, posthumous claims on his reputation by family factions did not help. Thrice married, Rice was not successful with love. His Pittsburgh wife divorced him and sought to seize his fortune while taking a younger man. His second marriage to an Erie, Pennsylvania 18-year old was stressed by familial and societal disapproval. He loved wife number 3, whom he met on a Texas lecture tour, but she stayed in Texas. Rice recalled his career late in life, embellishing at some times and fabricating at others. His memoirs were dutifully recorded by Maria Brown, who published his biography complete with the myths, lies and exaggerations. The mistruths were repeated by others until no one listened anymore. Then, even the written record faded.

This circus poster probably dates circa 1860s. Note Rice in the stars and stripes, perhaps a shred of evidence for the myth that he was the inspiration for Thomas Nast's "Uncle Sam." However, it is thought unlikely that Nast, an ardent Republican, would use Democrat Rice as a model. There were likely multiple "Uncle Sam" prototypes.

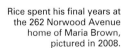

Rice spent his final years at the 262 Norwood Avenue home of Maria Brown, pictured in 2008.

The gateposts and porticos of *Brookside* are the most appealing features of an otherwise undistinguished house at 10 Norwood Avenue on the south side of Whale Pond Brook, the stream that separates Ocean Township from West Long Branch on the north. The original house, designed by Thomas Cressey and commissioned by Elisha Gaddis, both of Newark, and obscured beyond recognition by additions and alterations, was likely a 2 ½-story, side-gabled rectangular plan. The Gaddis' approximate 40-acre tract, earlier called *The Willows*, shrank to 5.2 acres by around the 1930s when it was owned by Isaac and Lena Alpern, who developed nearby Shadow Lawn Manor. Following Alperns' loss by foreclosure in 1938, *Brookside* was bought by New Yorkers Herman and Nettie Levinson, who occupied it seasonally until his death in 1959. After Nettie sold *Brookside* in 1961 to then-Monmouth College, the building initially housed their education department. Following a remodeling completed around 1962, *Brookside* has served as the residence of the president of the school, now Monmouth University. The house and gateposts are pictured in 1982 and 2008 respectively. After demolition of the old house, a 2008 reconstruction was reasonably faithful to the old one.

Golden Crest at 60 Norwood Avenue, also on the Ocean Township side, was built by Edward F. C. Young, one of Hudson County's leading businessmen of the latter 19th and early 20th centuries. Born in 1835, Young, although perhaps best known as president of Jersey City's First National Bank, was an officer and director of numerous substantial firms. This summer home was reportedly erected in only seven months, completed in May 1904, perhaps fast-tracked for his golden wedding anniversary with the former Harriet M. Strober, whom he married July 26, 1854. The architect of the house, pictured on a c.1910 post card, is unknown, claims of an attribution notwithstanding. Young died only four years after completion. *Golden Crest* was later a rooming house and then a fraternity house for nearby Monmouth College before being returned to residential use in the 1970s. (Courtesy of Glenn Vogel)

While the c.1912 post card suggests that Arthur Lipper's Elberon residence was named for his wife Clara, the back story is interesting. When this Philadelphian established Arthur Lipper & Co. in 1899 at age 22, he was the youngest head of a banking firm in the country. Clara was the widow of Asher L. Phillips, who built this Italian Renaissance Revival house, presumably not long after he acquired the property at the southwest corner of Ocean and Brighton Avenues, about a mile south of the Long Branch border in Deal, around 1905. Lipper bought the house from the Phillips estate, presumably to help satisfy bequests to other of his heirs. He stayed until his 1957 sale to Hathaway Homes. A modern house is on the site. (Courtesy Rutgers Special Collections and University Archives)

James. H. McVicker, a Chicago theatre owner, built *Meerschaum Villa*, his Second Empire house in 1868 on a large lot then extending deep to the south from the southwest corner of Park and Norwood Avenues, on the Ocean Township side of the latter. Schenck, who illustrated the house, claimed it was planned by the owner and built by George W. Brown of Long Branch. Perhaps peculiarities such as this Mansard should be expected when owners design. The house was renamed by a later, better-known theatrical figure, actress Maggie Mitchell who called it *Cricket Lodge* in honor of her best-known and widely acclaimed role "Fanchon the Cricket." She was Margaret Paddock when the house was bought in 1872, but later Margaret Abbott Mace, after her third husband, when it was sold in 1903. The place still exists, unrecognizable and totally covered through remodelings, but its original carriage house/stable survives, deep in the lot at 100 Norwood Avenue. As actor Edwin Booth was visiting while Pach photographed, he is seen at the doorway, while his child is in the hammock.

Well-known actor Edwin Booth married Mary McVicker in 1869, then built two years later this brick Second Empire house *Fairlawns* on Park Avenue adjacent to his father-in-law. Their short stay ended with its 1875 sale to publisher Thomas Talmadge Kinney. By the time of this c.1910 post card, the place was then the domicile of Kinney's daughter and William Campbell Clark of the Clark Thread Company, and renamed *The Oaks.* Demolished at an unspecified time, the lot is vacant in 2008. (Courtesy of Keith Wells)

Simon Guggenheim's Cottage, Ocean Ave., South Elberson

The soaring appeal of Elberon from the early 1880s occasioned the borrowing of the name to south of the Long Branch corporate limit. South Elberon was first mapped in 1886 from Poplar Swamp Brook south to Brighton Avenue and the ocean west to the tracks of the New York and Long Branch Railroad. By the time of the second expansion by the South Elberon Land and Improvement Company in 1903, the territory was part of the Deal borough, which was incorporated in 1898. Simon Guggenheim, 1867-1930, one of seven sons of copper magnate Meyer Guggenheim, built the Classical Revival house c.1900; it was probably designed by Brouse and Arend. The place was destroyed by fire March 31, 1915. The Guggenheims sold the property in 1925.

Henry B. Billings bought the corner portion of the divided Mace lot at Norwood and Park in 1902 for $10,500. Warrington G. Lawrence designed this fine Colonial Revival, a house with a rich interior not hinted by this c.1905 post card view, but depicted in the July 1904 *Architectural Record.* Four decades later the place was known as *Shady Rest,* but it was destroyed at an unspecified date. (Courtesy of Glenn Vogel)

After Samuel Sachs bought a lot west of Norwood (on the Ocean Township side) and north of Maplewood Avenue in 1900, he hired Joseph H. Freedlander to design this Italian Renaissance Revival house clad in cream-colored stucco and covered by a red tile roof. The verandas were partially enclosed and "architecturally related to the whole design," while the second story porch was "arranged for use." The house was extensively illustrated in the *Architectural Record* "Great American Residence Series" and published February 1903. The name *Ellen Court* was in honor of his daughter. It was reported the place was destroyed by fire in the early 1950s. (Courtesy Rutgers Special Collections and University Archives)

Leaving Long Branch on May 30, 2008.

Selected Bibliography

This list is representative of noteworthy works on Long Branch and Monmouth County.

Books

Buchholz, Margaret Thomas, Ed., *Shore Chronicles – Diaries and Travelers' Tales from the Jersey Shore 1764-1955,* Harvey Cedars, NJ, Down the Shore Publishing, 1999.

Busby, William, *The Oliver Byron Legacy – Showman and Builder*, Long Branch, NJ, the author, 2006.

Carlyon, David, *Dan Rice: The Most Famous Man You've Never Heard Of*, NY, Public Affairs, 2001.

Ellis, Franklin, *History of Monmouth County*, Philadelphia, PA, Evarts & Peck,1885

Federal Writers Project (American Guide Series), *Entertaining a Nation; The Career of Long Branch,* Long Branch, NJ, 1940.

Fischer, Robert J., *Norwood Park – An Exclusive Cottage Colony,* West Long Branch, NJ, West Long Branch Historical Society, 2000.

Flynn, Joseph M., *The Catholic Church in New Jersey*, Morristown, NJ, 1904.

Gabrielan, Randall, *Long Branch People and Places,* Charleston, SC, Arcadia Publishers, 1998.

Gordon, Thomas F., *A Gazetteer of the State of New Jersey,* Trenton, NJ, D. Fenton, 1834.

Hazard, Sharon, *Long Branch in the Golden Age,* Charleston, SC, The History Press, 2007.

Holmes, Frank, R., Editor, *History of Monmouth County* (3 Volumes), NY, The Lewis Historical Publishing Company,1922.

Kobbe, Gustav, *New Jersey Coast and Pines,* NY, Gustav Kobbe Co., 1891.

Long Branch Board of Trade, *Long Branch New Jersey,* The City of Long Branch, NJ, 1909.

Moss, George, *Double Exposure Two: Stereographic Views of the Jersey Shore (1859-1910) & Their Relationship to Pioneer Photography*, Sea Bright, NJ, Ploughshare Press, 1995.

Moss, George and Schnitzspahn, Karen L., *Victorian Summers at the Grand Hotels of Long Branch, New Jersey,* Sea Bright, NJ, Ploughshare Press, 2000.

Nelson, William, Editor, *The New Jersey Coast in Three Centuries,* NY, The Lewis Historical Publishing, 1903.

Pine, Alan S., et al., *Peddler to Suburbanite, The History of the Jews of Monmouth County, N.J.,* Deal Park, NJ, Monmouth County Jewish Community Council, 1981.

Schnitzspahn, Karen L., *Stars of the New Jersey Shore: A Theatrical History 1860s-1930s*, Atglen, PA, Schiffer Publishing, 2007.

Schenck, John H., *Album of Long Branch: A Series Of Photographic Views, With Letter-Press Sketches*, NY, John F. Trow, 1868.

Schenck, John H., *A Complete Descriptive Guide of Long Branch,* NY, Trow-Smith Book Manufacturing Co., 1868.

Snyder, John P., *The Story of New Jersey's Civil Boundaries 1606-1968*, Trenton, NJ, Bureau of Geology and Topography, 1969.

Van Benthuysen, Robert, *Crossroads Mansions – Shadow Lawn and The Guggenheim Cottage,* Turtle Mill Press, West Long Branch, NJ, 1987.

Wilson, Harold, editor, *The Jersey Shore,* (3 Volumes) NY, The Lewis Historical Publishing Company, 1953.

Directories

Boyd's, 1912
Polk's, various dates.

Newspapers

Asbury Park Press
Frank Leslie's Illustrated News
Harper's Weekly
Long Branch Daily News
Long Branch Record
New York Times
Red Bank Register

Monmouth Deeds

These are documents, not publications, but their familiarity is of inestimable help to researchers. While some early historical deeds may not have been recorded locally and may exist in other sources, the Monmouth County public repository of record is the Office of the County Clerk in Freehold. The use of deeds as a research tool has its pitfalls. First, few were recorded prior to the 19th century. Second, deeds document the transfer of land and rarely specify substantive information about structures on the land.

Index